PERRY'S DEAD!
(AND THE "JUICE" IS LOOSE)

OTHER BOOKS BY VICTOR A. FLEMING

Law, Literature & Laughter (hereinafter referred to as 'LLL') (1992)

A Briefer History of Time (unpublished)

Real Lawyers Do Change Their Briefs (1989)

Corpus Juris Thirdum (unpublished)

The Briefest History of Time (unpublished)

What You Should Know About Traffic Court (Before You Go In) (1978)

A Timed History of Briefs (unpublished)

A NEW LEGAL THRILLER
by
VICTOR A. FLEMING[1]

PERRY'S DEAD!
(AND THE "JUICE" IS LOOSE)

FOREWORD BY JUDGE JERRY BUCHMEYER

(includes reprint of Foreword to *Real Lawyers Do Change Their Briefs*,
same having been written by Hillary Rodham Clinton and Bill Clinton)

Artwork by John Deering

Little Rock: VAF "I Swear" Enterprises

---

[1]Author of *Real Lawyers Do Change Their Briefs*. (Yes, a
footnote on a title page *is* a bit unusual, but wait till you read
what is inside!).

Some material herein is reprinted from *Court Jesters*
by Peter V. MacDonald, with the permission of the
author and of Stoddart Publishing Co., Limited, Don
Mills, Ontario, Canada.
Some material herein is reprinted with the permission
of the National Corut Reporters' Association, Vienna,
Virginia.
Some material herein is reprinted from the "et
cetera" columns of Judge Jerry Buchmeyer in the *Texas
Bar Journal* and the *Dallas Bar Association Headnotes*,
with the permission of Judge Buchmeyer.

Author: Fleming, Victor A. (Victor Anson), December 26, 1951-
    Perry's Dead! (And the "Juice" is Loose)

ISBN 0-9649323-0-X

1. Law-Humor, facetiae, satire, etc.
2. Courts-Humor, facetiae, satire, etc.
I. Title.

L.C. Cat. No. 95-090937

Cover Design: H.K. Stewart Creative Services
                 Little Rock, Arkansas

FOR SUSAN

and in loving memory of
Elijah Anson Fleming, Jr.
and
J. Allen Smith

CONTENTS

Contents

"You can't think yourself into a new way of living. But you can live yourself into a new way of thinking."

—Fr. Richard Rohr

ACKNOWLEDGEMENTS

This book was no easy chore. I had help from many folks. I had support from friends and relatives, most of whom did not know what I was up to. They just put up with me as "the process" ran its course.

These` people, many of them unknowingly, were there to lend a helping hand, a caring ear, or a creative substitute title at times when the computer or other circumstances would lash out and try to subvert my carefully laid plans. *Perry's Dead!* was created in sporadic time bursts of energy (sometimes referred to hereinafter, if at all, as "STBEs")—often at the end or beginning of a day—late at night, or in the wee hours of the morning.

Acknowledgements are due lawyers, other professionals, and their aides and assistants who, knowingly or unknowingly, contributed to the contents hereof. Among them, without limitation, are

Tracie Bryant of Little Rock, Arkansas;
Judge Tom Bacus of Wichita Falls, Texas;
Kenneth Barron of Tyler, Texas;
David Beck of Houston, Texas;
Judge David Belew of Fort Worth, Texas;
Amy Bryant of Little Rock, Arkansas;
Judge Jerry Buchmeyer of Dallas, Texas;
John Buckley, Jr., of Galveston, Texas;
Faith G. Burk of Dallas, Texas;
Bryan Capps of Orlando, Florida;
Mitch Carthell of Amarillo, Texas;
Judge Jack Carter of Texarkana, Texas;

Graham Catlett of Little Rock, Arkansas;
Meredith Catlett of Little Rock, Arkansas;
Patricia Chamblin of Beaumont, Texas;
Judge David Cleveland of Palo Pinto, Texas;
John Cline of Snyder, Texas;
Robert Cloar of Fort Smith, Arkansas;
Larry Cotten of Forth Worth, Texas;
Leonard Cruse of Galveston, Texas;
Maudine Day of Little Rock, Arkansas;
Sonny Dillahunty of Little Rock, Arkansas;
Dick Downing of Little Rock, Arkansas;
Stuart Eilers of Cleveland, Ohio;
Guss Fennery of Astoria, Oregon;
Parker C. Folst, III, of Houston, Texas;
James Forbis of Decatur, Texas;
Tammie & Chris Foreman of North Little Rock,
        Arkansas;
Selina Frazier of Sherwood, Arkansas;
Carol Fritts of Little Rock, Arkansas;
J. Patrick Gallagher of Fort Worth, Texas;
Judge Catherine Adamski Gant of Fort Worth,
        Texas;
Chancellor Charles Garner of Fort Smith, Arkansas;
Kitty Gay of Fayetteville, Arkansas;
Mark Giles of Corpus Christi, Texas;
John P. Gill of Little Rock, Arkansas;
Desi Gipson of North Little Rock, Arkansas;
Lynne M. Gomez of Houston, Texas;
Judge James Gray of Orange County, California;
Barry Green of Fort Worth, Texas;

Acknowledgments

Milton Green (author of *It's Legal to Laugh*
    (1984));
John B. Hall of Houston, Texas;
E.P. Hamilton III of Austin, Texas;
Jon Hanna of Abilene, Texas;
Charles Harrison of Little Rock, Arkansas;
Fred Harrison of Little Rock, Arkansas;
Hugh Harrison of Jonesboro, Arkansas;
Albon O. Head, Jr., of Fort Worth, Texas;
Dr. Percy Heckman of Brazil;
Carol Barnett Heringer of Little Rock, Arkansas;
John Herrick of Fort Worth, Texas;
John Howie of Dallas, Texas;
Cliff Jackson of Little Rock, Arkansas;
Doreen Johnson of Edmonton, Alberta, Canada;
Marshall Jorpeland and the National Court
Reporters' Association, in Vienna, Virginia;
Yvonne Kemp, Manitoba, Canada;
Lisa Kilby of Bowling Green, Kentucky;
Dean Kilgore of Austin, Texas;
John Kirby of Dallas, Texas;
Becky Klempt of Laramie, Wyoming;
Kirk Kuykendall of Austin, Texas;
Michael J. LaValle of Phoenix, Arizona;
Edward W. Lavin of San Antonio, Texas;
Janice Law of Houston, Texas;
Al Ellis Lawyer of Dallas, Texas;
Richard Lederer (author of *Anguished English*
    (1987));
Mark Levbarg of Austin, Texas;

Lynn Lisk of Little Rock, Arkansas;
Wes Loegering of Dallas, Texas;
Peter MacDonald (author of *Court Jesters* (1985));
Ken Marks of Houston, Texas;
Steve Matthews of Pine Bluff, Arkansas;
Kay McClanahan of Little Rock, Arkansas;
James McGee of Phoenix, Arizona;
Thomas L. McGinnis of Cleveland, Ohio;
Ron McPherson of Houston, Texas;
Peter Miller of Little Rock, Arkansas;
R.K. Miller of Uvalde, Texas;
Judge James E. Morgan of Comanche, Texas;
Jimmy Morris (home unknown);
Drew Mouton of Big Springs, Texas;
Peter Myers of Riverside, California;
Joe Nagy of Lubbock, Texas;
Jennifer Naramore of North Little Rock, Arkansas;
Scott Nichol of Dallas, Texas;
David Noteware of Dallas, Texas;
Tom Overbey of Little Rock, Arkansas;
Thomas G. Pappas of Dallas, Texas;
R.D. Patillo of Waco, Texas;
Judge James Perry of Grand Prairie, Texas;
Judge Leon Pesek of Texarkana, Texas;
James C. Plummer of Houston, Texas;
Judge Henry Politz of Baton Rouge, Louisiana;
Brett Qualls of Little Rock;
Robinson Ramsey of Wharton, Texas;
Marilyn Rauch of Little Rock, Arkansas;
Richard Robinson of Irving, Texas;

Acknowledgments

Tom Rowatt of Houston, Texas;
Tommy Russell, late of North Little Rock,
  Arkansas;
John Sahlberg of Boise, Idaho;
Michael Setty of Pittsburg, Texas;
Clyde Siebman of Sherman, Texas;
Jimmy Simpson of Little Rock, Arkansas;
Cindy Singleton of Fort Worth, Texas;
Carolyn Dickinson Smith of Little Rock, Arkansas;
Clyde Siebman of Sherman, Texas;
Justice George Rose Smith, late of Little Rock,
  Arkansas;
David Solomon of Helena, Arkansas;
Tim Stanford of Dallas, Texas;
Barrett Stetson of Dallas, Texas;
Mary Strand of Tyler, Texas;
Judge Tom Sullivan of Houston, Texas;
Robert Summers of Austin, Texas;
Paul Taylor of Houston, Texas;
Richard A. Tindall of Houston, Texas;
Ira Tobolowsky of Dallas, Texas;
Rebecca Trammell of Lincoln, Nebraska;
Peter Tumin (author of *Great Legal Fiascos*
  (1985));
Richard Vining of Houston, Texas;
Gary A. Walters of Denton, Texas;
Judge Steve Wallace of Fort Worth, Texas;
Linda Watkins of Boise, Idaho;
Tim Watson of Newport, Arkansas;
Robert Weber of Texarkana, Texas;

Judge William R. Wilson, Jr., of Little Rock,
     Arkansas;
Mike Wilson of Jacksonville, Arkansas;
Gayle Windsor, late of Little Rock, Arkansas;
Judge David Young of Little Rock, Arkansas;
Jan Zanoff of Little Rock, Arkansas;
and many others here and there.

Additionally, I want to thank my current partners
and associates,[2] who abided the creation of this monster.

These acknowledgements would be incomplete if I
did not mention also John Deering, award-winning editorial
cartoonist for the *Arkansas Democrat-Gazette*, without
whose artwork *Perry's Dead!* would be a lifeless work.

Additional thanks are in order to Peter V.
MacDonald of Ontario, Canada, for some personal
consultation relative to the project and for his permission
to reprint freely from his first book, *Court Jesters* (Stoddart
Publishing Co., Ltd., Don Mills, Ontario, Canada, 1985),
which is now in its umpteenth printing.

I want to throw especial kudos in the direction of
U.S. District Judge Jerry Buchmeyer, who has been my
friend (and mentor) for several years and who has a greater
appreciation than do I for the real life occurrences in the
courtroom. The reason for this, as he will tell you himself,

---

[2]Which includes John Gill, Dub Elrod, Joe Calhoun, Judge
John Fogleman, Glenn Kelly, Heartsill Ragon III, Charles C.
Owen, C. Tad Bohannon, Robert Holitik, and Brad Sherman.

is that he is a judge (a *federal* judge) and, thus, in a position to see people make strange creatures of themselves while trying to do what they are supposed to do.

Also, he has given me permission to utilize items published first in his "et cetera" columns in the *Texas Bar Journal* and the *Dallas Bar Association Headnotes*. Many, many of the question-answer excerpts were originally published in Judge Buchmeyer's column, and most of those were sent to him by many of the people in the string acknowledgement above. I am most grateful to him also for his writing of the Foreword to this book. He is in good company, in that the Foreword to *RLDCTB* was written by a Mr. and Mrs. Clinton (*see* Appendix for reprint thereof).

Judge Buchmeyer is an intelligent and dedicated federal judge with a temperament suited to the position. Beyond that, he has a deep and abiding sense of humor, coupled with the ability to forego the temptation of taking life too seriously. He is a fine gentleman, as well, and I am proud to count him among my friends.

And last but not least I thank my son, Teddy Fleming, for assistance in coming up with the title to this work. That is a tale that must await another book for the telling.[3]

---

[3]Note that in "A Judicial Foreword," which follows these Acknowledgements, the footnotes are numbered independently. The folks at VAF "I Swear" Enterprises scholarly apologize for any inconvenience this creates for you Type A Obsessives out there.

"Unless you become as little children, you shall not enter the Kingdom."

—Jesus of Nazareth

A JUDICIAL FOREWORD

BY

JUDGE JERRY BUCHMEYER

This guy Vic Fleming has a Lot of Nerve!

Let me explain. There I was, several years ago, writing my monthly legal humor column (*"et cetera"*) for the Texas Bar Journal and the Dallas Bar Headnotes — collections of amusing, absurd, and/or laughable questions and answers from real trials and actual depositions — and regularly making the Most Humorous Speeches ever given anyplace, anytime by a United States District Judge.[1]

Then, in short order, this Victor A. Fleming guy from Arkansas sends a few marvelous(!) contributions for my columns — next gives me a copy of his first book (*Real Lawyers Do Change Their Briefs*), complete with license to reprint the funniest portions — and then, in 1991, invites me to speak at the Annual Meeting of the Arkansas Bar Foundation in Little Rock.

Vic introduced me, of course. Although I was reviewing my speech material during his introduction, I did

---

[1]A federal judge does not have an *ego deficit*.

notice that every remark he made about me (and my speech) drew riotous laughter. Well, this had the makings of the best introduction I had ever received, so I tried to respond in kind, beginning,

"Thank you, Vic, for that introduction. You know, of all the introductions I've had, that one — well, that one was certainly *the most recent*.

"Now, as Vic told you, I'm a Federal Judge, a Federal District Judge. But people on the U.S. Supreme Court are called 'justices.' Why is that? Why am *I* a 'Judge' — and why are *they* '*Justices*'? Well, the best explanation I've heard is this: There is no *justice* in the United States District Court — and there are no *judges* on the United States Supreme Court."

The audience roared! "Game, set and match to the out-of-town legal humorist," I thought, as I smugly delivered my patented All Purpose Universal Speech[2] to a great audience, probably my best ever. I was pleased, as Vic concluded the affair with heartfelt kudos and accolades. But then, as the crowd was leaving, this Arkansas lawyer from the audience shook my hand, smiled, and drawled, "*Judge, you were good, very good. But, you know that Vic Fleming, well — well, he's a Witty Guy! A really Witty Guy!!*"

I tried to ignore this "home-town review," and I returned to Dallas, where I was scheduled to speak to the

---

[2]Actually, I only have one speech—but I do have a number of different titles.

prestigious Southern Methodist University Air Law Symposium a few weeks later. This was a Really Big Deal — it was the Symposium's 25th Anniversary, and I had been specially chosen for a repeat performance, as their Very Favorite Speaker of all during the Symposium's first 24 years. Unfortunately, two days before the speech, I was forced to cancel because of some unexpected personal problems.

With less than 48 hours to find a substitute, the Symposium readily accepted my suggestion to invite Vic Fleming — and Vic, not knowing that this was a banquet address to over 500 aviation attorneys from all over the world, readily agreed to pinch hit. Well, as it turned out, Vic was a Smash Hit! My loyal staff, there for the speech, reported, "Vic Fleming is the *second* funniest legal humorist in the world." The SMU Air Law Symposium was grateful for (and somewhat amazed at) my ability to find a replacement of Rare Talent on such short notice.

So, things were good — at least until 1993, two years later, when I repaid my debt to the Air Law Symposium by appearing as that year's featured speaker. I was, to be candid, Absolutely Brilliant[3] — giving the very same 1991 speech[4] that wowed the Arkansas Bar Foundation crowd in Little Rock. The audience response was great, and once again I was pleased. But then, as the crowd was

---

[3]See footnote 1.

[4]See footnote 2.

Perry's Dead!

leaving, the Symposium Moderator (a *Dallas* attorney) patted me on the back, smiled, and drawled, *"Judge, you were good, very good, as usual. But that Vic Fleming, that Little Rock guy you got us two years ago, well — now there's a Witty Guy! A really Witty Guy!!"*

So, what can I do but agree? *Vic Fleming may have a lot of nerve — but he is, without question, a Very Witty Guy!* And he's more, much more: a dear friend and a kindred spirit, with an intense love for the legal profession and our judicial system — a love that Vic, too, expresses through wit and legal humor. I hope you learn that, above all, as you smile and laugh, and even guffaw your way through *Perry's Dead!*. As Vic concluded in his 1991 Air Law Symposium speech: "Next time you hear a tacky lawyer joke from a nonlawyer, invite that person to spend a few days in court with you. Stand up for your profession. Be proud of what you are. If we do not defend ourselves, no one else is going to do it for us. And, foremost, don't take yourself *too* seriously."

In her review of Vic's first book, Professor Frances Fendler of the University of Arkansas at Little Rock School of Law wrote, "I recommend *Real Lawyers Do Change Their Briefs* to any lawyer, to any lawyer's spouse, to any lawyer's parent, and to any lawyer's child who is considering following in Mother or Father's footsteps." These are my sentiments exactly about *Perry's Dead!*. But I must go

one step further: I would even recommend it to judges —
especially *federal judges.*[5]

Judge Jerry Buchmeyer[*]
October 1995

---

[5]See footnotes 1 and 3.

[*]Jerry Buchmeyer has been a United States District
Judge for the Northern District of Texas since December
1979. He has written a humor column, *"et cetera"* since
January 1979. In 1981 the Dallas Bar Association collected
his columns and published them in a book, appropriately
entitled *et cetera.*

"Know thyself."

"Nothing to excess."

(two inscriptions in stone at the temple of Apollo in ancient Delphi)

PREFACE

Perry's Dead

September 12, 1994, marked the end of an era. William Stacy—a Canadian born actor—departed this world at age 77. Stacy, better known by his stage name, Raymond Burr, was universally known as Perry Mason.

Although somewhat prepared for the demise of this American Hero (his health had not been good for some time), I was nevertheless shocked by the news. He left us at a time when his energy, his wit, and his brevity were sorely needed—*i.e.*, just before the commencement of the "Trial of the Century"—*People of California v. Orenthal James Simpson.*

The manner in which Perry disposed of cases in one TV hour during the 1960s remains the model for many attorneys: *Good v. Bad.* Brought out of retirement in the 1980s, Perry's cases were sensationalized into lengthier scenarios of *Bad v. Worse.* And then there was *People v. O.J.*

As the O.J. trial date neared, Burr died in an atmosphere in which lawyer-bashers were gaining ground. And in which some lawyers, and their clients, seem to relish legitimizing the bashers' repertoire.

"Perry's dead," someone said. "Can it be?"

"Yep," said another. "And the good will of the Bar ain't far behind."

The Juice is Loose

In October '94 jury selection began in the O.J. case. A year later—after the public debated DNA evidence, the prosecution's star witness was deemed an evil racist by both parties, and the Dream Team defense lawyers used rhyming couplets in their summation—the jury returned in less than half a day: "Not guilty."

The Juice is Loose! And a stigma has been etched onto the image of a profession. Some say it may be irreparable.

The Dream Team exuded offensive arrogance to many. The invidious, insidious Prosecution marched with high-minded self-righteousness. Both added to the shell from which attorneys must emerge to talk with others in society. So jaded are so many against "A" word professionals, that attorneys often cannot escape chastisement and insult among non-legal friends.

A *New York Times* editorial said the LAPD's errors turned "the mountain of evidence against Mr. Simpson [into] an eroding sandpile." Scott Turow, author of *Presumed Innocent*, called the People's case "a low road enterprise," saying prosecutors blindly accepted "unlikely stories from police officers."

Columnist Maureen Dowd wrote, "Any finale except instant acquittal capped by a clenched-fist salute from a juror who was once a Black Panther, anything other than the white van going down the *free*way while motorists cheered and waved would not have been artistically fitting for this Babylon tragedy-turned-farce that crystallizes everything warped about our society at century's end."

Columnist Thomas Sowell called for overhauling the criminal justice system by creating Professional Jurors, trained in law, anonymous, and immune from "being taken in by lawyers' tricks." The Simpson case, he said, "was a painful demonstration of what is wrong with the American legal system."

Ironic, isn't it, how critics take down the legal profession before, during, and after the notorious coverage, via TV, that they themselves demand! In my first book, *Real Lawyers Do Change Their Briefs* and my other writings, I have long pointed out that lawyers, first and foremost, are problem solvers, dispute managers, and business advisors. The legal profession is on the brink of unprecedented revamping *because of* an image—fostered by the O.J. trial and its ilk—that all lawsuits involve trickery, deceit, and manipulation and that, therefore, ethics and lawyers don't mix.

My forte has been to show the lighter side of business, law, and politics. That truth is stranger than fiction and funnier than jokes. In the wake of Perry's death and O.J.'s acquittal, a closer look at certain real-life aspects of law practice is once again in order.

1

MY MOTHER THE PROPHETESS

Don't ever slam a door; you might want to go back.
—Don Herold

My mother was a great Perry Mason fan. She got me hooked as a child. Some prophetic words of my mother return to me often:

Mother: You could be a great lawyer like Perry Mason, son, because you love to argue so much.

Me: I do not argue and I do not love to argue! And that's the last I want to hear about this arguing business!

*****

Years later, I applied to law school. I didn't realize lawyers would be the constant object of opprobrious epithets. And cruel jokes.

I vividly recall a day on which, among friends in a parking lot beside a golf course, someone (by accident, I believe), tried to close the trunk of a car while I was leaning in. After being restrained by one of the others, this fellow exclaimed, "Can you imagine anything worse than slamming a trunk lid on a lawyer?"

Someone piped up, "It might not be so bad. You might kill him."

Yet another voice chimed in, "Shakespeare woulda loved that!"

"Gimme a break!" I pleaded, trying not to seem argumentative.

Perhaps my mother had been onto something all along. *Is it possible that my training in English literature, and my knowledge of Perry Mason, is about to break forth in the context of automobile trunks and lawyer-bashing all at once? Nah!*

Mother, by the way, was never an O.J. Simpson fan. And, before the jury returned, she thought even Perry couldn't have gotten him off.

End of chapter. Short chapter. But they get longer. And deeper. But seldom are they argumentative. If you know what I mean. 'Cause I'm not an arguer. Right? I refuse to be. So, don't say that I am.

2

Bard No Barrister Basher

Ignorance is less remote from truth than prejudice.
—Denis Diderot

Echoing back to the chapter last past, folks who invoke Shakespeare around me are meddling. I, after all, am an English major, with significant Shakespearian training and affinity. And a Southern accent.

Few things rankle me as much as the supposed literary allusion to Shakespeare when the notion of killing a lawyer comes up. And when I get good and rankled, look out!

Newspaper writers have a special penchant for quoting the Bard out of all conceivable context. Back in the early '80s, when then-Chief Justice Warren Burger was lambasting lawyers right and left, railing about lawyer incompetence and lawyer advertising (and lawyer incompetence in lawyer advertising), no less a literary giant than the *Wall Street Journal* cited the infamous Shakespeare quote in such a way that it was clear the editorial writer hadn't a clue as to the proper context. The chief editorialist for the *Arkansas Gazette* did likewise, although he at least attributed the quote to "Shakespeare's character.

A couple of years later, a sports reporter for a Texas daily wrote, "As Shakespeare wrote it, King Henry

VI said: 'The first thing we do, let's kill all the lawyers.'...To Lord King Henry's hit list let us add college athletics' other latter day rapscallions, the sugar daddies and fat cat alumni."

Gimme a break! I shouted mentally, recalling the scene in the parking lot beside the golf course from years earlier. It was enough to make me want to argue. The Bard was not a barrister basher!

No one who insists on quoting that line from Shakespeare can correctly name the speaker.[4] It was not Henry VI. And that ain't argument. That's fact, with a Southern accent or otherwise!

When folks spew forth with the Shakespeare quote about killing all the lawyers, content to let it stand alone and suggest that all lawyers are rapscallions, I get more than seriously rankled. And tend to say things my mother would tend to call arguing.

I tend to call it setting THE RECORD straight.

In *The Second Part of King Henry the Sixth* (or *Henry VI, Part II*, for the non-purist), integral to the plot was a planned revolution headed up by the Duke of York. York enlisted Jack Cade as a "general." Cade was a low life rebel.

In one scene a messenger describes Cade's followers:

---

[4]Show me someone who can, and I'll prove that person does not *insist* on *quoting* that line! (He'll be quite content with a reasonably accurate paraphrase.)

His army is a ragged multitude
Of hinds and peasants, rude and merciless:....

Plotting secretly to become king himself, Cade says to his running buddies,

"There shall be in England seven half-penny loaves sold for a penny: the three-hooped pots shall have ten hoops; and I will make it felony, to drink small beer: all the realm shall be in common, and in Cheapside shall my palfrey go to grass. And when I am king,—as king I will be...there shall be no money; all shall eat and drink on my score; and I will apparel them all in one livery, that they may agree like brothers and worship me their lord.

Whereupon, Dick, the butcher of Ashford, speaks the infamous line: "The first thing we do, let's kill all the lawyers."[5] And, with the idea of bringing down the kingdom, Cade and his followers set out to kill all "scholars, lawyers, courtiers, [and] gentlemen."[6] Many of whom, without question, tried to argue them out of sallying forth with their mission.

None of whom were Perry Mason, who'd have respectfully requested that they cease, desist, and go hence

---

[5]Act IV, scene ii. In scene iii Cade says to Dick, "They fell before thee like sheep and oxen, and thou behavedst thyself as if thou hadst been in thine own slaughter-house:...thou shalt have a license to kill for a hundred lacking one a week." Behold thus the character whom many are so fond of quoting.

[6]Act IV, scene iv.

without day![7] None of whom were from O.J.'s Dream Team, who'd probably have represented Cade anyway.

[7] "Go hence without day" is an ancient phrase, used in legal pleadings to convey the notion that the judge should rule in favor of the party using the expression and that the other party should be sent on his way without his day in court. It derives from the Latin *sine die*, which means, literally, "without day," but connotes a final adjournment "without assigning a day for further meeting or hearing." BLACK'S LAW DICTIONARY (Rev. 4th ed. 1968). I Swear!

3

ARGUERS *v.* ATTACKERS

Why does a hearse horse snicker
Hauling a lawyer away?
—Carl Sandburg

As he was being badgered by some lawyers, in about 33 A.D., Jesus said, "Woe be unto you also, *ye* lawyers! for ye lade men with burdens grievous to be borne, and ye yourselves touch not the burdens with one of your fingers."[8]

This Bible verse is sometimes used out of context, although not nearly as often as the Shakespeare quote discussed in the previous chapters. A thorough study of Luke shows that the folks who were out to get Jesus were worthy of the reprimand.

Denouncing lawyers has been a popular pastime for centuries. The story is told that once at the offices of Sir William Jones, a British barrister of some note, a large spider dropped to the floor in the presence of Jones and a philanthropist named Day. Jones shouted, "Kill that spider, Day!"

---

[8]THE BIBLE, Luke 11:46 (King James Version).

Refusing to carry out the order, Jones's friend is said to have responded coolly,

"I will not kill that spider, Jones; I do not know that I have a right to kill that spider! Suppose when you are going to Westminster Hall, a superior being who, perhaps, may have as much power over you as you have over this spider, should say to his companion, 'Kill that lawyer; kill that lawyer!' How should you like that, Jones? And I am sure to most people a lawyer is a more obnoxious animal than a spider."[9]

An early example of a tacky lawyer joke (hereinafter referred to as "TLJ"). But the fun-poking at Jones lacks the universally demeaning aspect of the current stories that people pass off as "lawyer jokes."[10]

Clearly, things have gotten out of hand. So much so that it makes one—me, anyhow—want to argue. In my best Southern accent.

*****

---

[9]*Modern Eloquence* (1900), volume X.

[10]You know them all and I refuse herein to repeat them. But, so that you might have some sport of the matter, I'll give you just the punch lines to a few of the ones I have in mind:

(a) Deep down lawyers are okay.

(b) There are skid marks in front of the snake.

(c) "Professional courtesy."

(d) There are some things a white rat won't do.

(e) "Of course. Now, what's the second question."

"Americans love to hate their lawyers." I'll attribute that line to F. Lee Bailey, because I saw it in an article he wrote almost two decades before his involvement as a member of the O.J. Dream Team. But I'm sure he didn't say it first. Or think of it first.

In Bailey's opinion, "a lawyer's stock in trade is to attack people." It's one thing to *argue*, but *to attack* is a different ball game. Arguers seem to get by pretty well, I think. Attackers are not well liked by others at all.

The F. Lee Baileys of the world notwithstanding, the vast majority of lawyers are not professional attackers. And they don't aspire to evoking hatred in those about them. They spend most of their time analyzing and solving the problems of other people.

Lawyers, most of them, are human beings. They had childhoods. Many were kind to their mothers. Some had other aspirations before choosing law as a career. In many instances, character traits that are unfairly attributed to legal training have been with them since long before practicing law entered their minds.

America needs a concerted movement to depict accurately the ethics and activities of the average Real Attorney (sometimes hereinafter referred to as "RA"). There is a need for TV shows, films, books, magazines, and newspapers to inform the public that most RAs engage in many routine and mundane activities which their counterparts on the large and small screens never get around to because of the excessive glamour in their fictional lives.

At least, that's my theory. I shared my theory with my mother. She said I was arguing and suggested I write a book to set THE RECORD straight on this matter.

Obviously, I had to set her straight first. "I will do no such thing as write a book about this matter!"

"Okay, then," she said. "Don't write the book."

(Later she told me that if I changed my mind and did write the book, it should have some long chapters and some short chapters. Like she really knows.)

4

PROPOSED LAWYER APPRECIATION LAW

*I didn't like the play, but then I saw it under
adverse conditions—the curtain was up.*
—Groucho Marx

Television has emerged as this century's most pervasive and persuasive influence on public opinion. The main problem I have with TV is similar to Groucho's problem with the play: I watch it with the set on. The TV and movie image of lawyers leaves much to be desired.

From the latter "Perry Mason" shows of the '80s to "Matlock"; to "Hill Street Blues"; to "L.A. Law"; to "Law and Order"; to *Legal Eagles, And Justice for All, The Verdict, The Firm, The Client*; and *Jurassic Park*, lawyers are portrayed either as dishonest pseudo-geniuses who will do anything to outwit an opponent or imbecilic grab-baggers, out for the fastest buck available. These are not Real Attorneys (previously referred to as "RA"s), although the media coverage of such high profile trials as O.J.'s, the Menendez Brothers', Colin Ferguson's, and Susan Smith's do little to refute the inferences available to the public.

In movies and on TV lawyers who try to be ethical get thrown in jail. Seasoned litigators appear in each other's offices without appointments to read case law aloud. Every deposition results in either a shouting match or a fight. And this is not to mention the inter-firm, intra-firm, extra-firm sleeping around that gets in the way of folks' ability to cope with the pressures of law practice.

In this day of Court Television, every exchange among counsel becomes a battle in the view of the media. Changes in hairstyles become issues. Every potential wrinkle in every witnesses' testimony grows to proportions that are larger than life.

Art Buchwald wrote, "It isn't the bad lawyers who are screwing up the system—it's the good lawyers." But what about the fictional lawyers? There I go, arguing again.

*****

Rather than write the book, as my mother suggested, I decided to write a federal law. While it is true that some federal laws are longer than books, the one I wrote is not.

The Fleming Act of 1996 reads, "Before any person embarks upon a trade or profession, other than law practice, that person must first serve an apprenticeship of one year as an employee of a lawyer, a judge, or a court clerk." I figure this law's "popular name" will be "The Lawyer Appreciation Act."

Enactment of this law will mandate that the people who otherwise would be destined to become the harshest critics of lawyers and judges must first spend a full year observing them in action. The better to appreciate aspects of the justice system that millions never encounter.

Through these apprenticeships, people will learn how judges deal with cases in which the facts, the law, and the theories advanced are out of the ordinary. They also will ingest the manner in which RAs and litigants set forth, verbally and in writing, the essences of their cases. Or something like that.

The apprentices will gain a fuller appreciation of The Oath and its wondrous effects on normal people. Last but not least, these people will cease and desist with their TLJs. Maybe then Perry can stop spinning in his grave.

"TODAY THE WHITE HOUSE BEGAN REVIEWING BRIEFS ON VIC FLEMING'S LAWYER APPRECIATION BILL."

5

THE LAW IS A SUCK EGG DOG

*I have always thought of a dog lover as
a dog that was in love with another dog.*
—James Thurber

The gestation period of the inspiration heretofore
referred to in the chapter last past...
[SLAP, SLAP!
["Thanks, I needed that!"[11]]
... began while I was analyzing a particular case
years ago. It may come as a shock to you, but, because of
the way a particular set of judges handled a case almost
half a century ago, if you are having difficulty preventing
your neighbor's dog from sucking your fowl eggs, you can
hunt the dog down and shoot it with a certain degree of
impunity, if not immunity—in Mississippi, anyway.
According to the Supreme Court of Mississippi, "It
is...common knowledge that when a dog has once acquired
the habit of egg-sucking there is no available way by which

---

[11]I detest legalese, but have a tendency to fall into it from
time to time.

he can be broken of it, and...no calculable limit to his appetite."[12]

This judicially-made law emerged from a case in which the plaintiff's dog routinely went over to the defendant's rural homestead, bit holes in the turkey and guinea eggs, and sucked them dry. This tended to make the defendant more than just argumentative about the matter. The inevitable result was that two RAs got into the picture, and plaintiff sued defendant (irrefutable statistics show that more than 90% of lawsuits are started by the plaintiff suing the defendant).

The evidence in the trial had been that the defendant had tried to stop the varmint from this thievery. In several ways, all in vain. The high court of the Magnolia State understood how this failure could occur:

"[G]enerally [a suck-egg dog] has a sufficient degree of intelligence that he will commit the offense...upon every clear opportunity, in such a stealthy way that he can seldom be caught in the act."[13] Notwithstanding this obvious law of nature, the plaintiff had been arguing that the only method in which the defendant might lawfully eliminate the canine in question was to shoot it while it was doing its thing—the "to catch a thief in the act" doctrine. But to no avail, as the court resolutely stated:

---

[12]   *Hull v. Scruggs,* 2 So. 2d 543, 545 (Miss. 1941).

[13]Canines obviously have no innate appreciation of the cholesterol problem attendant upon this dietary plan.

"[W]e reject the contention [that] the dog could not lawfully be killed except while in the actual commission of the offense....After such a period of habitual depredation as shown in this case,...[one] is not required to wait and watch with a gun until he can catch the predatory dog in the very act. Such a dog would be far more watchful than would the watcher himself, and the depredation would not occur again until the watcher had given up his post and had gone about some other task, but it would then recur, and how soon would be a mere matter of opportunity."[14]

When I told my mother about the just discussed case, she allowed as how my going to law school must have been a waste of money after all.

"It was not," I replied—politely, not argumentatively. Wondering what Perry would say.

---

[14]*Hull v. Scruggs,* 2 So. 2d 543, 545 (Miss. 1941). It might be noted that, in so ruling, the Mississippi Supreme Court had some *obiter dicta* to which to look. For, in 1933, it had decided a case in which Ed Thomas had been indicted and convicted for stealing a cow and a yearling from Limon Minyard. The circumstances? Minyard shot and killed Thomas's dog after it had sucked Minyard's eggs dry for two months. Thomas then approached Minyard with a shotgun and demanded $20 as payment for the dog. Minyard not having a double sawbuck to answer the double-barrel on him, Thomas settled for the cow and the yearling, telling Minyard he might redeem them for $20. In affirming Thomas's conviction, the Court said, "Minyard was not guilty of criminal mischief in the killing of the dog....There is serious doubt as to Minyard's civil liability for the killing of the dog." *Thomas v. State,* 148 So. 2d 225, 226 (Miss. 1933).

"Well, what else did you learn in law school? Besides all this nonsense about egg-sucking dogs!"

"The phrase, Mother, is 'suck-egg dogs'."

That convinced me! The general non-lawyer public neither know nor appreciate that lawyers, as advocates for their clients, sometimes have, figuratively and literally, "dogs" for cases—not to mention (at least not yet) jackasses and one-eyed mares.

Yes, the Fleming Act apprenticeships will educate people about such cases. And demonstrate to them that, with professional skill and due diligence, attorneys must plead those cases. And argue those cases. And, with the help of witnesses, present those cases. And somewhere there are judges who have to decide those cases.

6

The Law is a Ass—or Related to One

If the law supposes that, the law is a ass.
—Charles Dickens' character, Mr. Bumble

Somewhere in 1915 there was Chief Justice Hall of the Texas Court of Civil Appeals, who issued a judicial opinion that was published in a hardback lawbook—as were the suck-egg dog cases from Mississippi. In it he described the humane destruction of the plaintiff's one-eyed mare:

"[S]he had been placed in the city pound and plaintiff was duly notified and failed to pay for her board, whereupon the city marshall employed one Jess, whose surname was Lemley, more familiarly known as 'Panhandle Pete,' who, at the direction of the mayor, ruthlessly took said mare's life by shooting her between the bad eye and the one not so bad. In other words, in the vernacular of gangland, when Panhandle Pete's pistol popped, she petered, for which the poundkeeper paid Pete a pair of pesos."[15]

My mother was but mildly amused by the Panhandler Pete case. So, for research purposes, from that moment onward, I began to try to ease my mother out of "the loop" on this project.

---

[15]*Canadian v. Guthrie*, 87 S.W.2d 316 (Tex.Civ.App. 1935).

*****

And so it was that I made no mention at all to her about the breach of warranty case, allegedly decided by a Judge Oliver and reported in a law book of some sort.[16] The plaintiff had purchased a jackass from the defendant and, being dissatisfied with the purchased product, had filed suit. He allegedly had discovered a major defect in the animal's "performance":

"The evidence before the court is amply sufficient to establish an express warranty on the part of the defendant that the animal in question was a fit and suitable one for breeding purposes, and the court therefore finds that there was a warranty. But even conceding that there was no such warranty, there surely can be no question, under the evidence, that there was an implied warranty as to its fitness as a breeder and foal-getter. The defendant must surely have known that the plaintiff was purchasing

---

[16]121 Neb. App. 72 is the cite given me for "Judge Oliver's Jackass Case." I've been unable to verify the existence of the source and extend an additional acknowledgement of gratitude to Rebecca Trammell and Carol Mutz (Ms. Trammell being the librarian at the University of Nebraska at Lincoln College of Law and Ms. Mutz being a law student there in 1993), who researched the issue of what, if anything, is "121 Neb. App." A mid-book acknowledgement should also be extended to Jacqueline Wright of the Arkansas Supreme Court Library, who came to the same conclusion as Ms. Trammell and Ms. Mutz—i.e., that there is no known source with the identification "Neb. App." But a technicality of this magnitude was deemed insufficient evidence on which to base a decision to excise the presentation of Judge Oliver's opinion. Or something like that.

the animal for breeding purposes only. He knew at the time of making the sale that no reasonable man would attempt to use a jackass for any other purpose than to outrage nature by propagating mules. He could not have supposed that the plaintiff desired to acquire a jackass as a pet. The animal is wholly unsuitable for that purpose. Its form is neither pleasing to the eye, nor its voice soothing to the ear. He is neither ornamental in his appearances, nor amusing in his habits; he is valuable only because he is able to propagate the mule species.

"It appears from the evidence that after purchasing the animal, the plaintiff on several occasions caused him to be placed in the society of certain soft-eyed, sleek-coated young mares, that were in the pink of condition which is supposed to arouse the interest and attract the attention of any reasonably amorous jackass, but that he passed them up and knew them not. The defendant admits representing to the plaintiff that the jackass in question would do the work for himself. But the evidence shows that if he was ever possessed of that valuable and charming accomplishment, he failed on the occasions just mentioned to practice it with the zeal and ardor becoming of an ambitious jackass in full possession of his faculties.

"He was, indeed, a worthless, unpedigreed and impotent jackass, without pride of ancestry or hope of posterity—a source of disappointment to his female friends, and an item of expense to his owner. There is no brute in all the animal kingdom more worthless than a Missouri-bred jackass afflicted with lost manhood. He was not as represented and warranted by the defendant, and the plaintiff is entitled to recover."

Even the Monday morning, non-lawyer Supreme Court Justice wannabe cannot argue with such astute reasoning.

*****

In my quest to verify the authenticity of the immediately preceding case, I was led to a hardback law book containing *State v. Jackson*.[17] This is a *keek-arse* case, if ever there was one. Pardon my Latin.

The relevant facts were that Mr. Jackson, in his pickup truck, encountered a police barricade as he was driving to a pasture where he intended to release his mule, which was in the back of the truck. Told that "no unauthorized traffic" could enter the area, by order of the sheriff, Jackson got the mule out of the truck, rode her to the pasture, released her, walked back to the truck, and was, under a Kansas statute, ticketed for refusing to comply with a "lawful order of [a] police officer...invested by law with authority to direct...traffic." Fortunately for us all, Chief Judge Foth of the Court of Appeals of Kansas did not limit himself to a discussion of the relevant facts:

"The animal involved here was named Frieda. Frieda's mother apparently had an impeccable equine pedigree—indeed, the events of this case suggest origins in the hunt country of Maryland or Virginia, with strains of hunter, Morgan, or perhaps saddlebred in her background. Unfortunately, like many young ladies of breeding she made a love match far below her station. Her mate may have had charm, and clearly had animal magnetism, but he

---

[17]5 Kan. App. 170, 613 P.2d 398 (1980).

was also indisputably a jackass. Frieda, the product of this unhappy union, was a mule." But the story gets better, as the jurist continues:

"She was no ordinary mule, however. Although genealogy and geography had conspired together to deprive her of her rightful heritage, Frieda could not be content with a mule's customary plodding fate, shackled to a plow or wagon, with no hope of pleasure in youth or even progeny to comfort her in old age. Encouraged by her owner and by a coonhound named Buck—reportedly valued at $1500—Frieda took up that nocturnal ritual known as coon-hunting. She was an apt pupil. From her father she had inherited a surefootedness which proved advantageous on rough and rocky ground. From her mother she had acquired talents which, with a little practice, enabled her to clear a four-foot fence with ease. It was this latter ability that precipitated the case at bar." (Nowhere in this reported case is it mentioned whether Frieda, or her lawyer, was adequately instructed as to the meaning of this historical phrase, "the case at bar." Until I got to law school, I thought it had something to do with a beer truck's delivery of inventory to a drinking establishment.)[18] Continuing with Judge Foth's opinion:

"It was in April of 1979, while returning from one of her favorite evening outings, that Frieda had her present brush with the law. It was almost midnight and Frieda, tired from the chase, was riding in the back of her owner's

---

[18]Not to be confused with the clever footnotes, this is the first of several tricky parentheticals (sometimes perhaps referred to hereinafter as "TP"s).

pickup, swaying gently between the stock racks and looking forward to spending the rest of the night peacefully in her pasture on the banks of the Verdigris River. Buck was in the cab with their mutual owner, the defendant. They had proceeded up the River Road to a point less than half a mile from Frieda's pasture when they encountered a police barricade and Deputy Lee Coltharp of the Montgomery County sheriff's office.

"...Although he had been allowed through some six hours earlier when he had picked Frieda up, this time the defendant was ordered to turn around and go back. He protested that doing so would mean eight or ten miles of driving to reach the nearby pasture, but Coltharp was adamant; it was 'Sheriff's orders.'

"Defendant...parked, got out, and signalled to Frieda. Obediently, Frieda jumped out of the truck. Before Coltharp could react, defendant mounted and rode off into the night, up the River Road, through the restricted area, to the pasture. There Frieda made her last leap of the night, over the fence and into the familiar safety of her home grounds.

"Defendant returned down the River Road afoot, again through the restricted area, to his truck and the waiting Buck. Also waiting was Deputy Coltharp, citation in hand."[19] Citing another Kansas statute, which defines

---

[19] 5 Kan. App. at 171.

"traffic" so as to include pedestrians and "ridden animals," the court affirmed the conviction.[20]

Okay. I understand the case, as I am sure you do also. But do you gotta feel sorry for the defendant in this case, or what?[21]

Reckon how long it would have taken Perry to persuade Hamilton Burger to drop this charge? The Dream Team, of course, would have demanded a jury trial. And, in summation, might have argued,

> *If he didn't drive,*
> *The charge don't jive.*

---

[20]Based on the irrefutable authenticity of Frieda's case, I hereby declare the jackass case also to be authentic, my inability to verify it through bibliographical resources notwithstanding.

[21]Please don't write me letters about my grammar. Having a degree in English from a good liberal arts college, I feel entitled to a presumption that deviations such as the one reflected by the noted sentence (yes, a *question* is a sentence) are intentional on my part, used for effect of some sort. A type of poetic license, if you will.

7

THE LAW IS MOJO AGAINST
SATANIC RADIUM BEAMS

Truth or fact? You have to choose.
Most times they are not compatible.
—Eddie Cantor

Having effectively eliminated my mother from the
loop, I never told her about the federal judge in
Pennsylvania who entertained a suit against Satan for
awhile before dismissing it on a technicality. Believe it or
not, Satan gets sued rather frequently in the American
federal court system.

In the case to which I have reference he was
accused of entering the heart and brain of the plaintiff and
causing severe mental and emotional anguish. Before
dismissing the case on the ground that the plaintiff "failed
to include with his complaint the required...instructions...as
to service of process," U.S. District Judge Weber opined
(in writing, for publication in a hardback law book):

"We question whether Plaintiff may obtain personal
jurisdiction over the Defendant in this judicial district....
While the official reports disclose no case where this
Defendant has appeared as a defendant, there is an

unofficial account of a trial in New Hampshire where this Defendant filed an action of mortgage foreclosure as the plaintiff. The Defendant in that action...raised the defense that the Plaintiff was a foreign prince with no standing to sue in an American court. This defense was overcome by overwhelming evidence to the contrary. Whether or not this would raise an estoppel in the present case we are unable to determine at this time."[22]

Asked about his motives in filing the suit in the first instance, the plaintiff probably said, "The devil made me do it."

*****

Another unusual federal case was filed in New Jersey, where anything can happen (and allegedly did). The plaintiff, in a pleading he wrote without assistance of counsel (I think), claimed he had been "taken to the Eye, Ear and Speech Clinic in Newark," and that while he was in custody, "the State...there unlawfully injected him in the left eye with a radium electric beam." Allegedly, as a result of this unsolicited medical treatment, he claimed that "someone now talks to him on the inside of his brain. He asks money damages of $12 million."

The quoted portions of the preceding paragraph are from the written opinion (in a hardback law book) of U.S.

---

[22]*U. S. ex rel. Mayo v. Satan & His Staff*, 54 F.R.D. 282, 283 (W.D. Pa. 1971) (I hope that I am insulting no one's intelligence by saying that the judge was referring to "The Devil and Daniel Webster").

District Judge Biunno. As are the following words, which the jurist utilized to dispose of the case:

"[T]aking the facts as pleaded, and assuming them to be true, they show a case of presumably unlicensed radio communication, a matter...within the sole jurisdiction of the Federal Communications Commission. 47 U.S.C. 151, *et seq.*"

(I pause here, pregnantly (though I am not pregnant), to assure you once again that I am not making this up. I am quoting from a hardback book that is full of federal case law, the kind of stuff that law students have to study to pass, the kind of stuff that will come to the eye of the general public only if the Fleming Act passes in 1996.) The judicial opinion continues:

"[A]side from that, [the plaintiff] Seawright could have blocked the broadcast to the antenna in his brain simply by grounding it. [Citation omitted.] Just as delivery trucks for oil and gasoline are 'grounded' against the accumulation of static electricity, so on the same principle Seawright might have pinned to the back of a trouser leg a short chain of paper clips so that the end would touch the ground and prevent anyone from talking to him inside his brain."[23]

Case dismissed. But chapter not yet over. Mojo case still to come. Plus two other implantation cases. Full sentences to be used again soon.

*****

---

[23]*Seawright v. New Jersey,* 412 F.Supp. 413, 414-15 (D.N.J. 1976).

I call *Seawright* an implantation case (it is Part I of a trilogy, actually). Not to be confused with *implant* cases, which involve breast enlargement or treatment for impotency.

There are a lot of implantation cases around, mostly in federal court—where the rules regarding *pro se* pleadings are rather liberal. And where people who believe their civil rights have been violated find a forum of competent jurisdiction.

Most implantation cases involve people who write their own pleadings. They have difficulty, I believe, finding lawyers who will represent them.

Implantation cases involve people who truly believe that someone, for whatever, reason, has secretly invaded their body and placed therein various devices. For some reason people who believe others have implanted electronic devices into their bodies think this is covered under civil rights law.

I represented a party in Case No. CV 89-6956 SVW in the United States District Court for the Central District of California. The plaintiff, a female, did a beautiful job of typing her own complaint. I assume she typed it herself because I have difficulty believing anyone else would have typed it for her. The suit was against five defendants: two of her former employers, the Little Rock, Arkansas, Police Department; the Pulaski County, Arkansas, Special School District; and the State of Arkansas. I quote from the complaint:

"While incarcerated for a traffic violation in a Pulaski County jail in Sherwood, Arkansas, a microchip of surveillance type was surgically implanted in Plaintiff's right ear. This implant was done without the written consent of myself or the courts. I went to jail on a Monday night and woke up on a Wednesday morning in time to be released to a friend who paid a fine of $190.00

"The surveillance started two days later. Their reason for the implant was 'to study my thoughts.'...The surveillance was done with a police band radio transmitter/receiver. This machine had 10,000 watts of power on me....The Sheriff's Department...destroyed four vehicles owned by the Plaintiff...: a 1976 Ford Granada, a 1978 Ford Granada, a 1974 Chevrolet Malibu, and a 1978 Ford Fiesta. All four vehicles resulted in faulty transmissions."

I assure you this is real. I have not made this up. It is in the public record in Los Angeles, California. The plaintiff sought leave of court to amend her complaint (once again with beautiful typing) several weeks after it was filed. From the proposed amended complaint:

"Plaintiff only knew of undue surveillance by the police and sheriff's departments and the occasional missing of personal items and monies. Plaintiff did not know that she and her family were being drugged with valiums in her water and food supply....Beginning in July 1987 said Defendants proceeded nightly to break and enter the Plaintiff's home and bring witnesses. Employees of past jobs, employees of past colleges, policemen, etc. were brought to the Plaintiff's home to harass and sexually assault her....Defendants had built their own secret entrance into the Plaintiff's trailer. If the Plaintiff slept at night, they came at night, if the Plaintiff slept in the daytime, they came in the daylight hours. Plaintiff could not find the secret entrance and tried blocking the doors with furniture....

"Proof [of the surveillance chip] can be seen on the dental x-rays of the Plaintiff....The power in the surveillance radio transmitter/receiver can be channeled to attack the Plaintiff's health in different capacities....Jolts of electricity create pains daily in Plaintiff's body. This device is glued to the Plaintiff's ear close to the brain and the skin acts as a good conductor of radio waves."

The amended complaint covered 13 pages, neatly typed and double-spaced, and concluded with "WHEREFORE, Plaintiff prays for an equitable judgment in the sum of SIXTEEN MILLION DOLLARS with interest for the harassing discrimination, loss of employment and suffering of the Plaintiff and her family...[and] such other relief as may be just and proper."

The complaint was dismissed for lack of subject matter jurisdiction, lack of personal jurisdiction, and improper venue, the district judge finding that "all of the alleged Title VII violations of which Plaintiff complains took place in Arkansas and all of the Defendants are Arkansas entities or persons."

*****

To complete the Implantation Trilogy, U.S. District Judge Jerry Buchmeyer, a friend of mine who also chronicles the humorous and the bizarre aspects of law practice in the modern world, reports that he was presiding over a competency hearing of a defendant who was "caught methodically breaking every glass door and window on the ground level of the federal courthouse in Dallas." At the hearing the defendant testified,

"The reason I did what I did is for sometime I have been tortured. I've been mutilated. I've been extricated from God and justice. The government, the veteran's administration, the CIA, and various defense departments colluded in gross criminal improprieties against me....[T]hey were poisoning me, injecting caustic material into my veins. Excruciating migraine headaches, nausea, burning of the eyes, uncontrollable bowels, visceral eruptions all over my body. Electrical devices have been surgically implanted —all these are telemetric. I've got leads right here with nuclear powered battery packs. I've got implants in my teeth...I've got maxillary sinuses. I've got enormous wiring in there attached to my genital nervous system."

At this point in the testimony, the assistant U.S. Attorney handling the case spoke up and said, "Okay. And someone is transmitting a signal which causes your sinuses to act up and you get headaches. Anything else?" Do you get the impression he's seen these symptoms before? The accused's testimony continues:

"Anything they can do. They—they, sometimes—well, sometimes they make me have an erection without probable cause—And that's all I have to say, your honor, and I appreciate you giving me the floor to say it."

After giving him the floor, the judge showed him the door.

*****

In yet another federal hardback law book, one can find a case where, to resolve a copyright claim over a popular song, it was first necessary to define...

...MOJO: "a collective noun used to describe one or more talismanic objects believed to have power intrinsic in their nature,... to impart power, or ward off evil...by being worn close to the body of...the person to whom the MOJO appertains. A simple example...would be a rabbit's foot. Other examples of MOJO, mentioned...in the trial record, include such amulets as black cat bones, shrunken heads, lodestones, half dollar with seeds...ashes, black snake skin, strands of hair and teeth. MOJO is often worn around the neck in a leather bag or carried on the person....[B]elief in MOJO naturally leads to the conversational gambit, 'Have you got your MOJO working?' or 'I've got my MOJO working.' A person approaching a crisis, such as an examination at school, would be sure to have his MOJO with him and working."[24].

Judge-made law such as that reflected by the above reinforced my resolve to go this project alone. My mother just would not have understood the mojo case.

(I wonder if Perry Mason had a secret mojo. Obviously, the Dream Team did!)

---

[24]*Stratchborneo v. ARC Music Corp.*, 357 F. Supp. 1392, 1396 (S.D. N.Y. 1973).

8

POETIC JUSTICES

I could no more define poetry than
a terrier could define a rat.
—A.E. Housman

"What in the world is this?" My mother and my wife were screaming, almost in unison. Somehow I knew they had come across my collection of judicial poetry. My mother was back in the loop! And had got my spouse involved in it as well.

From the corners of the continent I have assayed to collect legal documents written in or containing figurative language or poetry. All in an effort to compile the necessary portfolio of documentation for a successful lobbying effort on behalf of the Fleming Act. Among my collection is case law poetry.

According to yet another hardback lawbook[25], in 1973 a federal judge, Edward Becker of the Eastern District of Pennsylvania, set forth the facts of a particular case in verse, of sorts:

---

[25]*Mackenworth v. American Trading Transportation Co.*, 367 F. Supp. 374 (E.D. Pa. 1973).

A seaman, with the help of legal sages,
sued a shipowner for his wages....
The shipowner, in New York City,
subjected to long arm service without pity,
thought the suit should fade away
since it was started in PA....
In order for extraterritorial jurisdiction to obtain,
it is enough that the defendant do a single act
        in Pennsylvania for pecuniary gain.
And we hold that the recent visit of defendant's ship
        to Philadelphia's port
is doing business enough to bring it before this
        court.
We turn then to the constitutional point,
and lest the issue come out of joint,
so we now must look to the facts
to see if due process is met by sufficient "minimum
        contacts."
The visit of defendant's ship is not very old,
and so we feel constrained to hold
that under traditional notions of substantial justice
        and fair play,
defendant's constitutional argument does not carry
        the day.

I assure you, as I assured my mother and my wife
when I confessed these matters to them, that I am not
making any of this up. Even Judge Becker's footnotes were
in rhyme. For example,

> Long arm service is a procedural tool
> founded upon a "doing business" rule....

and

> That decision of the Supreme Court of Courts
> may be found at page 310 of 326 U.S. Reports.

*****

And of course there's Tax Court Judge Loe Irwin's decision in Twitty Burger, Inc.'s post-defunct-status trauma (referred to hereinafter, if at all, as "PDST") where the issue was whether money Conway Twitty repaid to investors in his failed burger business was tax-deductible?

Twitty had persuaded a host of country and western music stars and aficionados to invest in this fast food chain, which failed, miserably and quickly. Since the corporation had no assets, Conway repaid everyone who invested. He could afford it and he felt it necessary to preserve his reputation. But he wrote off the repayment as a business expense, and the IRS took exception.

Judge Irwin found a way poetically to rule:

> Twitty Burger went belly up
> But Conway remained true.
> He repaid his investors, one and all,
> It was the moral thing to do.
> His fans would not have liked it.
> It could have hurt his fame.
> Had any investors sued him,
> Like Merle Haggard or Sonny James.

When it was time to file taxes,
Conway thought what he would do
Was deduct those payments as a business expense
Under Section One-Sixty-Two.
In order to allow these deductions,
Goes the argument of the Commissioner,
The payment must be ordinary and necessary
To a business of the petitioner.
Had Conway not repaid the investors,
His career would have been under a cloud.
Under the unique facts of this case,
Held: The deductions are allowed.[26]

It's just an opinion (mine, in fact), but I don't think tax law was meant to be especially poetic. Not to be confused with the opinion of a famous legal scholar that "Judicial humor is a dreadful thing."[27]

*****

A case about damaged trees yielded more humorous (and more metric) verse, albeit a parody of an already established poem. Wrote Judge Gillis of Michigan:

We thought that we would never see
A suit to compensate a tree.

---

[26]*Jenkins v. Commissioner*, Tax Court Memorandum Decision 1983-667 (CCH Dec. 40,582M) (Nov. 3, 1983), n.14.

[27]Dean William L. Prosser, *The Judicial Humorist* (1952).

A suit whose claim in tort is prest
Upon a mangled tree's behest;
A tree whose battered trunk was prest
Against a Chevy's crumpled crest;
A tree that may forever bear
A lasting need for tender care.
Flora lovers though we three
We must uphold the court's decree.

The real problem in the cited example is that you cannot really tell what the case is about without reading the footnotes, which are far longer than the poetic opinion.

*****

And then there was Judge Goldberg of the Fifth Circuit Court of Appeals, who, in deciding *Anderson Greenwood & Co. v. NLRB.*,[28] felt obliged to cite two prior cases—*Clements Wire & Mfg. Co. v. NLRB* and *Robbins Tire & Rubber Co. v. NLRB*:

Our decision in *Robbins Tire*,
Interpreting Congress's reported desire,
Exposed workers to their bosses' ire.
The High Court, avoiding this sticky quagmire,
And fearing employers would threaten to fire,
Sent our holding to the funeral pyre.
Then along came *Clements Wire*,
Soon after its venerable sire.

---

[28]607 F.2d 322 (5th Cir. 1970).

To elections, *Wire* extended *Tire*
Leaving appellee's arguments higher and drier.
...We hope this attempt at a rhyme, perhaps two,
Has not left this audience feeling too blue.

It's been said that "if all the versifying justices were compelled to eat their own words, the punishment would be poetic justice!"[29]

*****

U.S. District Judge Thomas McBride of California was sharp enough to avoid writing poetry in the opinion deciding a case in which the defendant was charged with public nudity. But he could not resist quoting from the brief of one of the lawyers:

There was a defendant named Rex
With a minuscule organ of sex
        When jailed for exposure
        He said with composure,
"De minimis non curat lex."[30]

*****

---

[29]Smith, *A Critique of Judicial Humor*, 43 ARK. L. REV. 1, 11 (1990).

[30]Latin for the notion that the law does not concern itself with small and trifling matters. Although it was edited out of the TV screenplays, this phrase was regularly used by Perry Mason.

The following is the only example I have ever run across of a juror treating a courtroom to a poem.[31] It was the fourth week of a tedious trial regarding insurance coverage for a house fire caused by a certain brand of television. Two of 14 jurors had been excused.

In the days before *People v. O.J.*, this trial was considered lengthy and complex.

To keep matters from getting too mundane, the judge had passed the task of issuing the standard admonishment against discussing the case among themselves around among the jurors.

And on this particular day, the juror who volunteered, waxed poetic:

As the days of August slip away,
Here we sit in the courtroom of Judge James Gray.
We've had an earthquake,[32] a heat wave—
    two jurors are gone.
Today we came early. I got up before dawn.
We have each been asked to advise our group
Not to discuss this case while eating our soup,
To beware of statements vague and unclear,
And to keep in mind only facts held so dear.
So take careful notes and stay awake.
This is serious business; lots of money's at stake.
Keep an open mind, don't come to conclusions.

---

[31]I refuse to let the fact that it really doesn't fit in with the previous literature of the chapter deter me from printing it here.

[32]Yes, this is a California case.

Don't snap to judgments for fear of delusions.
Try to be patient, all things come to an end.
Someday soon we'll be home with our family and
      friends.
So enjoy your time off, get something to eat.
Drive carefully, avoid trains, till next time we meet.

Those were the days, I guess. Must have been. We
saw nothing of this sort from the O.J. jury. Let's meet
again in the next chapter.

9

ON HILLBILLIES AND MANURE

When a husband and wife have got each other,
the devil only knows which has got the other.
—Honore de Balzac

We meet again. As planned at the end of last chapter.

Message: Not all legal poetry rhymeth.

In 1960 a Judge Roark sat on the Missouri Court of Appeals. To him was given the assignment of opining as to the definition of an "Ozark hillbilly." He did so poetically, but without rhyme.

It all began in Stone County, when Lowell Moore, a rural mail carrier, filed for divorce against his Avon saleslady wife, Minnie. He alleged as grounds for divorce "general indignities." The divorce was granted by a lower court, and Minnie appealed.

According to Judge Roark's written opinion (and again, we are talking about something from a hardback law book, something which I did not make up), Lowell "in all sincerity" asserted that the Four Freedoms recognized in Stone County included "the right of a man to be master in his own house, the right of a man to fish and hunt with his friends at reasonable times without interference from the wife, and the right to deal and trade in livestock without the wife's intervention."

Minnie was alleged to have unreasonably interfered with Lowell's freedom on quail hunts, turkey shoots, and fishing trips. "To use a southern Missouri expression, she wanted to tie the stake rope a little too short." The most troublesome allegation, however, was that Minnie had taken to name-calling where Lowell's relatives were concerned. Yes, she had repeatedly referred to them as "hillbillies." On appeal the critical issue was whether or not this was an "indignity."

In resolving the issue, Judge Roark opined, *inter alia*[33], as follows:

"An Ozark hillbilly is an individual who has learned the real luxury of doing without the entangling complications of 'things' which the dependent and over-pressured city dweller is required to consider as necessities. The hillbilly forgoes the hard grandeur of high buildings and canyon streets in exchange for wooded hills and verdant valleys. In place of creeping traffic he accepts the rippling flow of the wandering stream. He does not hear the snarl of exhaust, the raucous braying of horns, and the sharp, strident babble of many intense voices. For him instead is the measured beat of the katydid, the lonesome, far-off complaining whippoorwill, perhaps even the sound of a falling acorn in the infinite peace of the quiet woods. The hillbilly is often not familiar with new modes, soirees, and office politics. But he does have the time and surroundings conducive to sober reflection and honest thought, and the opportunity to get closer to God. [I]n

---

[33]This is a legal term that translates basically to "What you're fixing to read is not all of what was originally written."

Southern Missouri the appellation 'hillbilly' is not generally an insult or an indignity; it is an expression of envy."[34] Case dismissed.

Is it ironic or what that at the same time Lowell and Minnie were squabbling in the Show Me State, Messrs. Gomez and Dykes were having at it out in the Grand Canyon State? With the somewhat less than poetic result that the Supreme Court of Arizona was asked to decide whether cow manure is real estate or personal property. In true judicial fashion, the court, drawing upon centuries of common law, found a way to hold that sometimes it is one thing and sometimes the other.

Ownership of the manure in question was the issue. One party had sold to the other a ranch and, as part of the transaction, had leased back the right to leave cattle on the property for feeding and roaming about and otherwise engaging your basic bovine-type activity. Like moo cow tea parties. And brahma bull bull sessions.

The party whose cattle were feeding on the property came over and, apparently as a matter of course, removed 1645 tons of manure from the feed pens. The fellow who had bought the ranch put a stop to this activity and then shoveled out 660 tons for himself.

At about this point in the recitation of the facts, my mother said that she did not care to hear anymore about this case. My wife and my sister were laughing their heads off. "Bullfeathers!" said my sister (one of the nicer comments). "You're making this up," my wife said.

---

[34]*Moore v. Moore*, 337 S.W.2d 781, 789 (Mo. App. 1960).

I told them, as I have told you, the reader, several times now: "This is true stuff. Not make believe at all! The Real Thing!"

The court ruled, and correctly, I believe, that cattle dung is real estate when it is produced by animals being fed products grown on the land in question. But if made "otherwise than in the usual course of husbandry, it forms no part of the realty...but is regarded as personal estate...." If animals are not fed products of the land, the land is not impoverished. The owner then has "no duty to leave the manure to replenish the land." In a rental situation animal manure that is "in no sense the product of the demised premises...is not part of the realty and may be removed by the tenant at the close of his term."

Now, here we have a rule of law that every lawyer in America should be fully cognizant of. BS can be real property or it can be personal property. It all depends upon the transaction that precedes the bowel movement. A Legal Gem if ever there was one!

The court awarded to the seller/tenant the entire 660 tons of manure removed by the buyer/landlord, valuing the manure at $2.50 per ton. A claim for punitive damages was dismissed.[35]

Essay question: What is it about animal excrement that makes human beings (a) think stories about it are funny; (b) want to use the various phrases that describe it in their everyday speech; (c) get into courtroom battles over owning it; and (d) all of the above?

---

[35]*Gomez v. Dykes*, 82 A.L.R.2d 109 (Ariz. 1961).

Lest you think I dare end this portion of the book with a case bottomed on bovine bowel movements, I want rather to conclude with a couple of rodent stories—one in text and one in a Most Sincere Footnote (referred to hereinafter, if at all, as "MSF").

In 1971 inmates in the Suffolk County, New York, jail petitioned for a show cause order. The warden's agents had flushed, literally (as in down the toilet), a "professional mouse" named Morris whom, or which, they had discovered in a cage in one of the plaintiffs' cells.

The judge actually inspected the cell block before ruling on the case, which included a constitutional claim that Morris had been denied due process by being discriminatorily discharged without a hearing. The court's written opinion began by dismissing the constitutional claim because Morris, not having signed in as a jail visitor (and not being an inmate as such), was not entitled to be on the premises:

"The court, upon signing in as a jail visitor, took judicial notice that Morris had never fulfilled this requirement. He apparently was a trespasser and could accordingly be ejected by such force as was necessary, although not by excessive force. It does not appear that the water pressure in the jail is excessively forceful."

In conclusion, however, the judge (probably also an English major) poetically sympathized with Morris, using the famous words of Robert Burns' 1785 poem "To a Mouse (on turning her up in her nest with the plow)":

> I'm truly sorry man's dominion
> Has broken Nature's social union
> An' justifies that ill opinion

Which makes thee startle
At me, thy poor, earth-born companion.
An' fellow mortal!...
The best-laid plans o' mice an' men
Gang aft a-gley,[36]
An' lea' us nought but grief an' pain,
For promised joy.[37]

*****

The MSF referred to above is about to occur. It has
to do with a lively gathering in my living room, in Little
Rock, Arkansas, in 1987, when three lawyers and one
investment banker were sharing tales of life and work. A
scenario which, around me, has tended in years since
1984,[38] to involve at least one or two recounts of
"humorous" legal incidents.

One of the other lawyers told of her defense of a
national company that processes, packages, and sells food
in a civil suit in which the plaintiff claimed that while
cooking a can of the defendant's vegetables, the lower half

---

[36]"Gang aft a-gley" means "go oft awry."
But do nae ask me how or why.

[37]*Morabito v. Cyrta*, N.Y. Sup. Ct. (Suffolk County, Aug.
26, 1971) (as cited in Buchmeyer, "et cetera," Dallas Bar
Headnotes, Feb. 17, 1987). Poetry cleaned up via *The Norton
Anthology of English Literature, Revised* (1968), vol. 2 at 26-28

[38]1984 being the year in which I began writing a column of
legal humor for Arkansas lawyers.

of a small rodent boiled to the top of the pot. Causing severe mental anguish and emotional distress, of course.

"What's so funny about that?" asked the investment banker.

"Nothing, really," said the first lawyer, "except that for months around the office we called it our *rat's ass case*."[39]

What followed, as I recall, was one of those three-minute periods during which no one could stop laughing.

---

[39]Obviously, I was one of the lawyers. The lawyer who told the story was First Lady Hillary Rodham Clinton. The other lawyer was President Bill Clinton, then-Governor of Arkansas. The investment banker was my wife, Susan. That conversation led to a pledge on the Clintons' part to write a foreword for my first book. The pledge was fulfilled. *Real Lawyers Do Change Their Briefs*, which was in the publication process at that time, was released in 1989. The Clinton Foreword ("CF") is reprinted in the Appendix hereto, for no reason other than that I'm still proud of them and it!

10

KALI THE ALLEY CAT *v.* LITTLE THUNDER JIM

*It ain't no sin if you crack a few laws now
and then, just so long as you don't break any.*
—Mae West

And then there are the pleadings. These are the documents that are filed in court. Through which and by which litigants allege, aver, and contend ("AAC") that their opponents are in the wrong and they alone are in the right. Pleadings were seldom quoted on "Perry Mason."

Thus, the general non-lawyer public, including my mother, doesn't really understand pleadings. Neither do many of the media pundits who are so fond of writing of them or talking of them in their publications or on their networks. The two basic pleadings are the "complaint" and the "answer," although one will find deviations throughout time and space. Once the two basic pleadings are filed, barring motions to dismiss and the like, it is said that the "issues are joined."

Among many other laudable goals of the Fleming Act is to ensure that the attorney-critical lay public come to know how certain issues must find their way to the brink of actual litigation. How issues in unusual cases (and in some usual cases) come to be joined.

In 1980 a complaint filed in Lonoke County, Arkansas, alleged that the plaintiff was "the owner of a Tree Walker hunting dog named Little Thunder Jim, which was duly registered with the United Kennel Club in Kalamazoo, Michigan," and that the defendant "did wilfully and without provocation shoot the aforementioned dog, while the same was lawfully on the premises of the plaintiff, thereby causing his death." Syntax[40] notwithstanding, it was Little Thunder Jim, not the plaintiff, who died on plaintiff's premises. A professional hunter, plaintiff claimed that Little Thunder Jim provided "a portion of his livelihood" and sought damages of $10,000.

In the answer, after a half page or so of generally denying any liability, the defense lawyer set forth the following as an "affirmative defense":

"1. Little Thunder Jim was an uninvited intruder on defendant's homestead and Little Thunder Jim had repeatedly been told to leave.

"2. Little Thunder Jim, at the time of the incident, was standing over and attempting to molest a small female, whose name is Baby, that resides at defendant's homestead

"3. Defendant admits that the resident female may have led Little Thunder Jim, and others like him, to believe that Baby was a loose female; however, defendant denies that Baby was loose enough for the likes of Little Thunder Jim.

---

[40]*Syntax* means sentence structure, with a focus primarily on word order, and should never be confused with *sin tax*, the levy placed by government on gambling, liquor, tobacco, etc.

"4. Defendant had a right to protect all females on his homestead from unwanted suitors."[41]

Talk about a dawg of a case!

*****

And what could be more appropriate than to follow such a canine conniption with a feline catastrophe. Of sorts.

In May of 1988 a jury in Jonesboro, Arkansas, took up discussion on the case of Kali, the alley cat. (And, once again, I swear and affirm that I am not making this up—even though I confess to be writing the following in an overtly clever manner.)

It all began when Konni Clayton's neighbor, Mr. Kemp, killed Konni's cat, Kali. In the complaint Konni claimed Kali had ventured onto Kemp's lawn and that when Konni later called for Kali to come home, Kemp without cause "did in fact shoot the cat with a gun in front of Konni...at least three times, causing the death of the cat." Konni claimed 50,000 clams for her anguish over Kali's killing.

Kemp did not categorically deny the killing, but rather sought to justify it, claiming, in the answer, that

---

[41]*Lamb v. Davis*, Lonoke County, Arkansas, Circuit Court No. Civ. 80-28. Although Mike Wilson, a long-time Arkansas legislator, is acknowledged in the Acknowledgments section of this book, I want to acknowledge him a second time here because he sent me the Little Thunder Jim pleadings and, by the time I first published them in my magazine column, I had misplaced his transmittal letter and forgotten who had sent them to me—thus, I omitted to give him due credit earlier and want to double up now.

Kali was "laying in wait under one of [Kemp's] bird feeders." Determined to deter the cat, Kemp pleaded, he fired a pellet gun in the "general direction of the cat and the pellet accidentally struck the cat."[42] Continuing to plead, Kemp claimed that, upon ascertaining that Kali was "mortally wounded, he shot her twice more to relieve her suffering."

The jury awarded Konni $250, apparently the aggregate of her adoption fee from the Humane Society and an estimate of the cost of cat food during the cat's life.[43]

"Rats," said Konni's counsel, who was hoping for a bit more of a poultice to cover her wound—and his fee.

Speaking of rats...

---

[42]The record is silent on whether the pellet showed any remorse.

[43]Clayton v. Kemp, Craighead County, Arkansas, Circuit No. CIV 87-531.

11

FROM MOUSEBURGERS TO MAGGOT BARS

The penalty for laughing in a
courtroom is six months; if it were
not for this penalty the jury would
never hear the evidence.
—H.L. Mencken

Animals tend to get implicated in alleged civil wrongs in other ways than overtly making nuisances of themselves to the neighbors of their owners. With occasional grisly results in the pleadings. And lawyers have been known to try to soften the grisliness with, of all things, a sort of poetry.

The day before Halloween in 1986 happened also to be the last day before a particular statute of limitations was about to run out on a products liability claim involving animals. On that day there was filed in Pulaski County, Arkansas, Circuit Court, by a lawyer who was never accused of not thinking very highly of himself. The animals involved were soft-bodied, grublike, footless insect larvae. The complaint read as follows:

1. Deborah Jean Surber, a Little Rock lass
(A devoted chocolate addict, alas)
Trotted down to her friendly Alco Store
Her Hershey supply to restore.

2. Now Hershey's, a company in Pennsylvania,
Sells candy worldwide (even in Transylvania).
And way down south in Ar-Kansas
(In the Alco Stores, headquartered in Kansas)
There wiggled on the shelves some Hershey's
          candy.

3. 'Twas 1983 on Halloween night—
Ghosts and goblins everywhere in sight—
But the sickest apparition Deborah ever would
          see
Was inside the wrapper of the Hershey's candy.

4. There wiggling and squirming all over the
          place
Were oodles of maggots, flavoring the taste,
Adding protein to every bite she would take
(Except those who sneaked off her plate,
And a few straggling souls who, though a mite
          late,
Came stumbling and crawling from her mouth as
          she ate).

(I am pausing here to emphasize that (1) I know this is the
worst poetry ever written by a human being, even a

lawyer, and (2) I am not making this up.) The complaint
continues:

> 5. Deborah shrieked in horror and practically
>   fainted—
> She had no idea that the candy was tainted—
> After all, there were the company guarantees
> Of expressed and implied merchantabilities,
> And of fitness for the particular purpose,
> To-wit, to eat it, for which she'd purchased it.
>
> 6. But somehow Hershey in stirring this batch
> (Or maybe it was Alco on its shelves, alas)
> Thought ghosts and goblins were not sufficient—
> On this Halloween they would be negligent
> By adding all those squirming worms and
>   maggots
> (Well—maybe not so many, just a few to gag
>   us).

(I solemnly swear *and* affirm that I am not making this
up—not even parts of it.) This pleading goes on (and on
and on):

> 7. So off to the stores in original packages
> Munched oodles and gobs of crunchy maggots;
> And off to the doctor, her stomach a-heavin',
> Her bowels a-movin' and her food all a-leavin'
> Went Deborah Jean—a reformed chocolate
>   addict.
> Let the jury decide what should be the verdict.

WHEREFORE, when Deborah Jean prays,
and pray now she must,
She seeks what is right, that which is just,
A green poultice to cover her wound,
Say somewhere in the tune—
of two million dollars.
(Won't the Defendants Holler!)
Of compensatory and punitive damages
        aggregated
(You see, she's just a mite aggravated),
Plus interest, of course, and court costs, too,
Just to make it worthwhile to bring this suit.

Duckwall/Alco retained a firm of highly qualified attorneys for the defense, and the Real Lawyer who drew the assignment of initially responding to the complaint, not to be outdone by the instigator of this legal literature, responded in kind to the plaintiff's allegations:

All material charges lack substance and pride;
as related to Duckwall/Alco—are hereby denied.

She failed to allege any damage ensued;
merely that she has a weakness for food.

Assumption of risk she had clearly accepted
by eating the candy she knew was infected.

Any defective status was quite clearly shown
by the "oodles" of critters, so she should have
        known.

(On stacks and stacks of Bibles *and other religious books*, I promise I am not making this up. Cross my heart and hope to die, stick a needle in my eye.) The answer continues:

> Any harm that resulted from plaintiff's ingestion
> was caused by her biting without an inspection.
>
> She therefore is guilty of taking the fault,
> no proximate cause, her lawsuit must halt.
> No facts to support lack of fitness for use;
> pleads no cause of action and cooks plaintiff's
> goose
>
> Under Arkansas statutes the Complaint is amiss
> and due to such failure, it should be
> dismissed.[44]

Several months after the foregoing pleadings were filed, I asked one of the lawyers how the case had come out and was told that the case had been settled on terms that must remain confidential. Although tempted to argue, I just said *"Gomez v. Dykes"* under my breath and went on with life as I know it.

*****

As should be obvious from the foregoing, it is not a crime to plead in rhyme. Which brings me to a complaint

---

[44]*Surber v. Hershey Food Corp., et al*, Pulaski County, Arkansas, Circuit Court No. 86-10266.

authored by a Riverside, California, attorney in a suit against a nationally-known fast food restaurant:

> 1. Plaintiff names here as his foes
> a group of persons who're called Does,
> the names of them from one to ten
> are not quite yet within his ken....
> But so their blame will not be eased
> nor they past liability squeeze,
> he names them and if the court please
> will amend and set their names out stark
> when he's no longer in the dark....
>
> 10. ...Some like pickles, some like relish,
> some say, "Hold them, please."
> But plaintiff never ever said,
> "I'd like mousie with my cheese."
> Yes, it was mousemeat broiled and ground
> which plaintiff's tummy did surround,
> the taste of which he could not manage,
> which caused the soon-to-be shown damage....
>
> 18. But did defendants ever say,
> "We may have mice, so stay away"?
> Or warn the plaintiff and the rest of us:
> "These rodents have got the best of us"?[45]

---

[45]*Gilbert v. Wendy's International, et al.*, Riverside County, California, Superior Court No. 157070.

Again, I assure you, I am not making this up. The complaint goes on a bit more (and, from the numbers, you can tell there is much that I have omitted. I never found out how the case came out. And I never mentioned any of the above and foregoing to my dear mother.

I'm wondering whether Perry Mason ever encountered a *rodentia en cuisine* case. As for the O.J. case, there were plenty of rodents involved there.

12

THOSE *PRO SE* PLEADERS

Only exceptionally rational men can afford to be absurd.
—Allan Goldfein

The joining of the issues takes on an entirely different flavor from time to time. That is, when the pleader herself writes her pleadings without assistance from a lawyer. Seldom (except in small claims court) does a case go forward without at least one side being represented by counsel. And, faced with a *pro se*[46] pleader, counsel occasionally plays along.

Once on behalf of a department store client of his, an RA of my acquaintance filed a collection suit in municipal court against a woman, seeking judgment for $165.23, the amount alleged to be due on an installment contract having to do with the purchase of a washer and dryer. Appearing *pro se*, the defendant responded, *inter alia*[47], as follows:

"I have done everything in my power to pay my bill....I am suing this Company for harassment, and mental anguish, for One Hundred Thousand Dollars, and Twenty-

---

[46]Legal lingo meaning, in essence, "for self."

[47]*See* note 33, *supra.*

"I have done everything in my power to pay my bill....I am suing this Company for harassment, and mental anguish, for One Hundred Thousand Dollars, and Twenty-Five Thousand Dollars for punitive damages and asking that all other debt be resolved here and now and that Forty-Five Dollars and Eighty-Five cents that was paid for warranty be returned to me for I had them out eight times to fix my washer and dryer and they are not fixed today, they do not work right....

"Now, if and when I have a court hearing, I will have proof and more. It is time someone stopped Old Toads like plaintiff's attorney, the poor and the needy have suffered because of someone like him. I will see you in court."

The very day he received this pleading my friend filed in the clerk's office a document which stated,

"The defendant, representing herself, refers to the plaintiff's attorney as an Old Toad. Plaintiff takes exception to such characterization, which is totally inaccurate and misleading. Plaintiff's attorney, in fact, is an Old Frog, and is patiently awaiting the day when a beautiful princess will kiss him and transform him into a handsome prince."

The defendant's claim for $100,000 had the effect of bumping the case automatically to a higher court for a jury trial. The final result, after a trial to a twelve-person jury, was a judgment for the department store in the amount of $165.23.[48]

---

[48]*J.C. Penney Company v. Richards*, Pulaski County, Arkansas, Circuit No. 85-1494.

****

The following is from a pleading entitled "Original Petition for Divorce," written in longhand and filed, for Public Record, in Harris County, Texas:

"Respondent..., who knows all, tells all, and sees all..., that wonderful and delightful person whom petitioner loves with all his heart[49] despite it all, is a 'TRANSIENT PERSON' and may be served with process where she may be found....

"These parties were joined together in HOLY MATRIMONY [in 1983]. They ceased living together as Husband and Wife on January 21, 1984, when she got PISSED OFF and HAULED ASS with the car, the Mastercard, $350 cash, her FEDERAL CIVIL RIGHTS NINE-YEAR-OLD EMPLOYMENT DISCRIMINATION CASE against...the Texas Department of Human Resources, to which she is WELCOME, having BORED ME STIFF for two years about just how everybody picks on Kathryn....

"Petitioner prays that CITATION and NOTICE issue as required by LAW and that the Court GRANT A DIVORCE and Decree and such other and further relief as requested herein, including changing Respondent's name to Bella Abzug, Jr., and for...

[Here there are drawings of trumpets and drums.]

---

[49]Actually, instead of the word "heart," the petitioner here had drawn a little heart-shaped figure.

"...TA-TA-TA-TAAA...STAND BACK, IT'S ALMOST HERE—ED MCMAHON IS ON STAGE NOW—

"HEEEERE'S GENERAL RELIEF—

[Here there is a drawing of a package of Rolaids.]

"(Screw you, Bitch, I filed first and your suit is subject to a plea in abatement.)

"Respectfully submitted,...."[50]

A thorough review of this pleading left me speechless. Nearly. For awhile...

*****

...Until I saw this next one. In the Little River County, Arkansas, Chancery Court, an inmate of the Arkansas Department of Correction filed a suit in 1990. In a "Civil Complaint" against the local prosecuting attorney, the plaintiff alleged as follows:

"Plaintiff...challenges the acts of governmental functions by the defendants herein as they be so contrary to the Arkansas State Constitution of 1874 under the provisions of Article 2 and Article 7 as each may be seriatim in the complaint at bar."

(I am not making this up.) The complaint continues:

"[A] lawful impanelled jury convicted the plaintiff of Capital Murder, and sentenced him to life in prison without parole. The court rendering the conviction herein consisted of: [here the complaint names the judge, the

---

[50]*In re the Marriage of Paul Frank Hensler, Petitioner, and Kathryn Patteson Hensler*, Harris County, Texas, No. 85-4521.

prosecutor, a deputy prosecutor, and the court reporter, all of whom have the same last name[51]. Each of the named court officials participating in the case at bar are all invuikatuib of Arkansas State Constitution of 1874, Article 7 section 20, which states as seriatim:...'No judge or justice shall preside in the trial of any cause in the event he may be interested, or where either of the parties shall be connected with him by consanguinity or affinity, within such degree as may be prescribed by law'."

The complaint then goes on to describe the familial relationships of the named individuals. Had enough? It ain't over yet. The answer of the defendant states, *inter alia*:

"Defendant is not conversant with the word 'invuikatuib,'...and would ask for a definition of same."

Whereupon the plaintiff, in a responsive pleading of sorts, states: "...Defendant not being conversant with the word 'invuikatuib' should research the definition and respond to Plaintiff."

I'm not certain, but I am guessing that the plaintiff was being somewhat invuikatuibish himself in his responsive pleading.

*****

Religion has been known to play a role in how the *pro se* folks respond when they get sued. Consider the

---

[51]Readers in Little River County, Arkansas, and surrounding areas may successfully guess the names of these individuals, to whom apologies are hereby made for any inconvenience this notoriety may cause them.

following *pro se* answer filed in Phillips County, Arkansas, Chancery Court divorce action:

"The Defendant Mal Stokes, Jr., by his attorney, Jesus Christ, for his cause of reaction, states [*inter alia*] that during the marriage of the parties the Defendant has loved the Plaintiff [and] the Defendant has pardoned the Plaintiff.

"WHEREFORE, Defendant...prays that he be not granted an absolute divorce from Plaintiff...and all other relief to which he may not be entitled.

"/s/Mal Stokes, Jr., Candidate for Justice,...Spokesman for his Attorney."[52]

The attorney who originally sent me the above pleading was representing the plaintiff. He sent me the pleading for purposes of seeking my advice on a ticklish ethical matter: "Shall I file a motion [alleging] that Defendant's attorney is not licensed to practice in Arkansas?"

*****

The following enlightening legal literature is the answer filed by some defendants who were alleged to owe some tax money to the United States government. Apparently they resided in Kansas, but you be the judge:

"We object to plaintiff's attempt to attach personal jurisdiction to Gladwin and Anna Lamb....[P]ersonal jurisdiction can only be made within the VENUE for which it is prescribed....Without PERSONAL JURISDICTION,

---

[52]*Stokes v. Stokes*, Phillips County, Arkansas, Chancery No. E-92-35.

no **PREAMBLE INHABITANTS** can be coerced by order
resulting from the pretended service of process....The State
of Kansas, as defined by its Constitution, in comparison to
the statutory district of Kansas, as defined by
Congressional Statute, shows the Lambs are outside the
VENUE of your jurisdiction.

"FOR TAX PURPOSES, OUR SOVEREIGN SPHERE
OF AUTHORITY IS URANUS.... "

"These two **VENUES** are completely different
legally. To make it understandable, one must pretend there
are two areas known as Kansas which are exactly alike
geographically, although each contains different inhabitants
and property in a legal sense. The part that is confusing is

that, in reality, there is only one land mass known as Kansas....

"The [Lambs] are within the VENUE defined by the Kansas Constitution, for KANSAS INHABITANTS, for Sedgwick County. The VENUE outside Kansas' boundaries, as defined in its Constitution,...is the INTERNAL REVENUE CODE THAT...authorizes the President to define INTERNAL REVENUE DISTRICTS for taxpayers, IRS agents...and other persons;.... INTERNAL REVENUE DISTRICTS are VENUES established for administration of INTERNAL REVENUE LAWS....

"The Lambs, who are persons in a COMMON LAW VENUE, have no legal connection to the IRS law [and] the process goes beyond its statutory regional VENUE.... This is what is meant when courts say that each of the STATES and the UNITED STATES are SOVEREIGN within their own sphere of authority.... 'SPHERE OF AUTHORITY' and VENUE mean about the same thing. The Lambs move for dismissal for lack of jurisdiction.

"Without Prejudice,

"/s/ Gladwin C. Lamb, Anna E. Lamb, Preamble Inhabitants of the Posterity, Wichita, Sedgwick County, Kansas."[53]

---

[53]*United States v. Lamb, et al.*, U.S.D.C. (D. Kan., Wichita Div.) No. Civ 89-1533-C. I doubt the Lambs were aware of a not totally dissimilar situation's being reported in *Price v. United States*, 798 F.2d 112 (5th Cir. 1986). Convicted of failure to file tax returns, Price pleaded that he "is a 'Dejure citizen of the

The above pleading was sent to me by an attorney who noted in his transmittal letter, "And you thought you understood civil procedure." I never understood quite that much civil procedure. But the Lambs' discourse leads to the trivia question: "In which sphere of authority did Dorothy and Toto preambly inhabit?"

*****

Here is an excerpt from some answers to interrogatories in a personal injury case. Answers to interrogatories are sort of like a pleading and sort of like sworn testimony. Usually, they are more like a pleading because the lawyer "crafts" all the language. In this case, however, the lawyer apparently was wise enough to allow someone just to transcribe the plaintiffs' actual words (you will, I think, be able to tell that I am not making this up):

"INTERROGATORY NO. 1: Please state the names and addresses of all doctors you have seen for examination or treatment of the injuries alleged by you in the Complaint.

"ANSWER: This is the sad part of it. We are poor people. We earn just enough money to live on. We did not have any money to pay for high-priced medical services and had to suffer it out, taking aspirin, using Sloan's liniment. We tried everything. We used Heet liniment,

---

State of Texas, under principles of jus sanguinis and jus soli' and that 'his STATUS is different than most of the automatons inhabiting our lands today.'" Care to guess the result?

Watkin's liniment and rubbing alcohol. We used the alcohol to cool off with when the liniment got too hot.

"...INTERROGATORY NO. 3: State the amounts of all doctors, nurses, hospital, medical and drug bills incurred by you because of the injuries alleged in the Complaint. Please attach to your Answers to these Interrogatories copies of such bills.

"ANSWER: It never did occur to us that we would have to submit an itemized statement for the aspirin and liniment. We were hurting so bad we just rubbed it up. We were not thinking about the liniment and aspirin but were just trying to get some ease and rubbing so we could sleep at night. When you are nervous after being struck like we were, nothing will do you much more good than stretching out on the bed and having somebody rub you from top to bottom, and if they rub you long enough, you will go to sleep and then you won't hurt anymore till you wake up."

I hope the plaintiff's lawyer found a way to read that answer to the jury. Because I still get a tear in my eye when I read it.

*****

And finally (for this chapter anyhow), there is the following pleading, entitled "Statement of Issue by Respondent and Acknowledgment," which was filed in response to a complaint that sought to collect on a student loan:

"Comes now Defendant, James A. Fountain, as per representative, and acting in his own defense declare the following testimonial statements in the alleged complaint filed by plaintiff in writing, under oath, and in accordance with Arkansas rules of civil procedure:...

"II. That Defendant so acknowledges: that Plaintiff alleged complaint to the indebtedness of $9,440.61...of student loan presented in complaint or thereto is aphorismic in its contentions.

"III. That Defendant so acknowledges: to the Court that presently I'm employed at the United States Postal Service main facility as a casual worker at $5.00 per hour of which you incur 50-60 hours per two week period or less. A casual is without formal tenure and can be laid off after a given number of tours.

"Further advise the Court that my unpunctilious redress for payment with specific respect to this indebtedness was due to an unstable market for hiring availability as well as an economy that has circumscribed itself to strictures of predilection for students in the humanities.

"IV. That Defendant so acknowledges: that I've been ordered by the Court to pay child support for five (5) children in the amount of $200.00 per week along with other represent annuities.

"—utilities (gas, light and phone) in the amount of $200-270 monthly.

"—Rent is $245 per month of which I'm presently 6 months behind.

"—Presently I have no transportation.

"—Presently own no real or personal property.

"V. Defendant so acknowledges: that I have unequivocally without delay made the plaintiff and its representatives aware of categorical impediments for equitable redress. And further affirm that specification on my financial status, employment, etc. has always been available for judgment and investigation. Defendant will also attest that this has been provided through the years and conveyed in letters and verbal communication to its agents and representatives.

"Wherefore, Defendant prays that when judgment is rendered by the Court that it will offer lateral unabridgement with specific understanding that this Defendant wishes honorably as plaintiff to seek recovery without malice, and will endeavor to work toward that end. Defendant further prays and hopes that the court will specifically with prudence weigh the materiality of facts, illustrated by the Defendant in his petition and grant his desire to dispel any unfounded hypothetical inquiries without justifiable merit defined in law.

"Lastly, Defendant prays for obeyance by the Court that will permit me to respectfully seek out financial closure. A financial plan for restructure to pay or make payments on the indebtedness in six months from today, subject and defined by the Court for review periodically when it deems permissible for ethical redress."[54]

On that note, this chapter will become laterally unabridged.

---

[54]*Arkansas Student Loan Authority v. Fountain*, Pulaski County, Arkansas, Circuit No. Civ. 91-517.

OPPORTUNITY TIME!

At this point in your current reading experience, the folks at VAF "I Swear" Enterprises would like to hear from you. And to supply you with other products available at present. Please clip on the dotted line below and return your order to us with your comments. Allow three weeks for delivery.

TO: VAF "I Swear" Enterprises   Comments:
FROM:

_____
(Name)

_____
(Street Address)

_____
City, State, Zip Code)

<u>Order</u> <u>Quantity</u> <u>Description</u>   _____ <u>Price</u>

___ *Real Lawyers Do Change Their Briefs*   @7.95   ___

___ *Law, Literature & Laughter*   @5.95   ___

___ *Perry's Dead! (And the Juice is Loose)*   @11.95   ___

___ "Restoring the Image of Lawyers"
     (audiotape)   @10.95   ___

Subtotal: _____
Add the greater of $2.00 or
5% postage and handling: _____

Total: _____

Checks payable to VAF "I Swear" Enterprises,
3801 TCBY Tower, Little Rock, Arkansas 72201

13

FROM NIGHTINGALES TO INVEIGLED PROTUBERANCES

If you can't convince them, confuse them.
—Harry S. Truman

The more things change, the more they stay the same. In his summation to the O.J. jury, defense counsel Johnnie Cochran waxed poetic, using repetition of a rhyming couplet: "If it doesn't fit / you must acquit." Consider now an excerpt from a closing argument in a federal criminal trial in Mississippi from the mid-1980s:

"Ladies and gentlemen, if He who made the moon and the sun and hung the stars on high could be merciful and just, then so can you. I submit to you ladies and gentlemen of the jury that if you convict my client on the testimony of thieves, rogues, whores, and disgruntled politicians, that never again will the nightingale of a clear conscience perch upon your pillow to sing you to sleep at night, but that the ghosts of the wicked and the perjured shall be your companions until your dying eyes shall turn to read the rapt and mystic meaning of the stars."[55]

---

[55]The jurist who sent me this piece said that it took the jury three minutes to convict the defendant, two minutes of which was spent electing a foreman.

*****

Back to written pleadings, the type that RAs with flair tend to write. Among the types of cases that used to be rather common, especially during and following times of war, was the suit by one man against another for "alienation of affections." In the mid-1950s, a complaint was filed in Sebastian County, Arkansas, Circuit Court:

"Comes the plaintiff, Bob Crain, and for his cause of action against the defendant, Louis Jackson, states and alleges:

"...Plaintiff and Neva Crain were lawfully married within the confines and jurisdiction of this Honorable Court on or about the 3rd day of July, 1951, A.D., with a duly constituted and elected Justice of the Peace officiating. Louis Jacobson stood by and with the plaintiff, Bob Crain, and did then and there act as what is commonly called and known in matrimonial parlance as 'the Best Man.'

"Plaintiff and his said bride did, in due time, enter into and consummate their respective marital and conjugal rights and duties, all to their mutual enjoyment, benefit, happiness and bliss. Said marriage did continue to exist in a joyful and happy state and was so continuing and existing until the defendant, by various nefarious enticements and subtle inducements and influence did invade the hallowed precincts of the castle of the plaintiff and his wife, and did wilfully, maliciously and without justifiable cause forever sever those sacred ties binding plaintiff and his wife, thereby alienating her affections form him and depriving plaintiff of the aid, comfort, conjugal affections, happiness, society and consortium of his wife and the loyal union between them existing. All of the said defendant's clandestine acts and activities in seducing and debauching plaintiff's wife were calculated, occasioned, carried out and fulfilled while plaintiff was loyally serving in the uniform of his country on foreign shores and while plaintiff was without the means, nearness, weapons and opportunity to defend the portals of his halcyon home. The said defendant's intents, motives and nocturnal desires were satiated only after plying plaintiff's wife with intoxicating beverages, heaping upon her grandiose and expensive gifts and using many other esoteric artifices practiced by a self-styled Lothario and fascinating deceiver of women to such an extent that the said wife of plaintiff succumbed to those carnal desires made infamous in the Garden of Eden by Adam and Eve."

(I give solemn oath: I am not making this up. It is in the Public Record in Sebastian County, Arkansas.) The complaint continues:

"After having so loyally and competently served his birthright, flag and nation within foreign boundaries, plaintiff was returned to this country for the purpose of receiving an honorable discharge and arrived in Fort Smith, Arkansas, at or around 1:00 o'clock A.M. on the 4th day of April, 1954, and after reporting to his superiors at Camp Chaffee, Arkansas, went to his supposed home...at or around 3:00 o'clock A.M. on said date, and did then and there find the love-nest created by the defendant actually being used by said defendant and plaintiff's wife in an illicit manner. The said plaintiff, his suspicions aroused by whispers and rattling of change in a man's pants pocket, did enter the front door of [the home] and did then and there observe the defendant making a rather rapid and hurried exit through the rear door of said place and out into the all enveloping darkness of night. Said exit was made so speedily that defendant was forced to leave parked for the time being a rather valuable piece of personal property, to-wit: a 1953 Coupe DeVille Cadillac, and was thereby force to return later, at an unseen moment, for same.

"After his wily ways had enabled him to inveigle his protuberances into the heart, body and soul of plaintiff's once-loving wife, the defendant prevailed upon her to correspond with plaintiff and advise him that she no longer loved him and did not wish to continue their marriage. The said correspondence was written while plaintiff was still outside the continental limits of the United States of America, and while the plaintiff was also corresponding with what once was his Best Man and best friend, to-wit: the defendant.

"After diligently employing those products of Bacchus presently distilled and fermented by Seagram and Gilbey; after heaping upon her gifts not to be afforded on a PFC's wages and after conjuring and using other methods and means, practiced since man first pushed aside the proverbial fig leaf, and after prevailing upon the plaintiff's wife to advise plaintiff that she no longer loved him and did not wish to continue their marriage, the said plaintiff's wife did on the 6th day of April, 1954, file an action for divorce and said case in now pending.

"All of said defendant's acts and activities, done, committed and entered into wilfully, maliciously, deliberately and without justifiable cause, brought about such a mental and physical condition to plaintiff that he has been forced to undergo pain and suffering to such an extent that he is subject to blackout periods, cannot eat or sleep and is without orientation as to his status and standing in the world and will so continue to suffer. And further, plaintiff has been subjected to the ridicule, contumely, ignominious and contemptuous regard of his neighbors and friends. For all of which plaintiff has been damaged in the sum and amount of $100,000 as actual damages and by reason of the defendant's wilful and malicious acts, plaintiff should have and recover from the defendant the further sum and amount of $100,000 as punitive damages."

The lawyer who drafted the above pleading told me that the case was tried to a twelve-person jury; that his client was awarded a substantial judgment (though he did not say how much); and that he collected from the defendant the entirety of the judgment.

*****

Occasionally, a lawyer pleading for her client, makes a run at having flair and falls just a bit short. Consider the following, from a response to motion for default judgment:

"Modern federal practice favors trials on the merits over default judgments. [Citations omitted.] A review of the case law shows a marked reluctance on the part of federal courts to grant default judgments except in the most gregarious instances. [Citations omitted] This is not an instance that warrants a default judgment."[56]

I guess she meant that it was not a particularly friendly atmosphere. Let alone gregarious.

---

[56]*Keeling v. International Paper, Inc., et al.*, U.S.D.C. (E.D. Ark.) No. LR-C-90-540.

*****

And whether the lawyers in the following exchange were gregarious with one another or not I am unsure. The first, it might be argued, was somewhat egregious. For, after the plaintiff amended his complaint to bring in a party that the defense had contended all along was a necessary party to the suit, in a "Reply to Plaintiff's Response to Motion for Summary Judgment" she alleged, *inter alia*:

"Apparently plaintiff did finally decide to make allegations against the only party possibly at fault, however, reluctantly."

Normally, a reply to a response to a motion is the last document filed in a series. But that did not stop the plaintiff's lawyer in this case from filing a "Replication to Reply to Plaintiff's Response to Motion for Summary Judgment," which reads *in full* as follows:

"The undersigned, one of the lawyers for Plaintiff, opines that the last sentence in the first paragraph of [the]Reply to Plaintiff's Response to Motion for Summary Judgment is rather snippy."

I believe Perry Mason would have enjoyed that pleading. Whether O.J. Prosecutor Christopher Darden would have is another matter altogether.

Speaking of other matters, did someone say, "Let's move on"? Okay, let's, let's, let's...

14

CHILLA MAKUSA
V.
GEOPOLITICAL RELATIONS

*A sense of humor keen enough to show a man his own
absurdities will keep him from the commission of all sins
...save those that are worth committing.*
—Samuel Butler

...Let's digress for a chapter and discuss a certain
need that arises occasionally in the true world of the RA.
The world as to which the average non-RA has so little
appreciation in this, the pre-Fleming Act era.

There are times in the RA's practice when she feels
she must inject some degree of humor and creativity into
the otherwise starkly dull areas of her practice. Which is
another way of saying that occasionally one must say or do
something a little bit differently than normal, lest she swell
up and bust!

Many lawyers are reluctant ever to succumb to this
most healthy of inclinations. And many, it is fair to say,
just cannot pull it off successfully. (But so what? They
could give it their best shot and then throw away the paper!
Or quickly apologize, if contempt stared them in the face.
They'd feel better for it. Read on!)

The story is told of a young member of the New York bar, who was noted for his sarcasm when excited, and also for his sense of humor and his quick wit. While engaged in the management of a tough jury trial, this young gentleman, in the presence of the judge and the jury, quoted the biblical proverb, "Cast not thy pearls before swine."

Vis-à-vis the judge, the lawyer had not done so well, and it was obvious he was nettled at the repeated rulings of the court against him. As counsel rose to give his summation to the jury, the judge facetiously remarked, "Be careful that you do not cast your pearls before swine."

"Don't be alarmed, your honor," came the quick reply, "I am about to address the jury, not the court!"[57]

*****

An especially dull (and often depressing) aspect of law practice is the contacting of clients who, for whatever reason, have not paid their fees. In 1983 Little Rock, Arkansas's William R. Wilson, Jr.—having not yet become the U.S. District Judge he is now—had represented someone in circumstances that allowed him to submit his legal bill to the City. The bill went unpaid for a few weeks and, in early December, a copy of a letter, on Bill's letterhead, arrived at City Hall. It was addressed to Bill's children and the address on the letter was that of a local, and well-known orphanage.

---

[57]*Modern Eloquence* (1900), vol. X.

Dear Children:

I so much regret chastising you because I know you are so anxious to get out of the orphanage. Unfortunately, however, I cannot provide even the most meager home and victuals for your little growing bodies until [the City Attorney and City Manager] send me payment for our statement which they promised so long ago.

Yes, these are the same people that you have heard me mention so many times, referring to them as high-type individuals, A-1 individuals with the nicest sense of personal honor, and on and on. No, children, their appointment secretaries advise me that they will be in the Bahamas during the Christmas season and neither will be able to play Scrooge in the orphanage play.

Yes, I did succeed in having their union cards pulled as Santa Claus protagonists. No, children, please don't try to call me anymore. My phone has been disconnected by the telephone company, and my neighbors are tired of coming to get me when you call. Furthermore, I emotionally cannot stand to hear your lonesome, hungry little voices until we can once again be united.

cc: City Manager & City Attorney[58]   Love,
                                              Dad

---

[58]This letter was previously published in *Real Lawyers Do Change Their Briefs*.

He received a check shortly thereafter. And probably sent a thank-you note to the City. Perry Mason would have done that. Or at least had Della Street handle the matter for him. The Dream Team, I think, might have called a press conference to address the issue.

*****

No post-1988 discussion of the topic of humorous legal correspondence would be complete without mention of the infamous letter from Laramie, Wyoming's Becky Klempt.

In search of a California attorney to collect a judgment she had obtained for a client locally, on July 19, 1988, Becky wrote Steven G. Corris of Irvine, California:

Dear Mr. Corris:

This firm obtained the enclosed judgment against ...Stephen H. Broomell on June 4, 1987. The judgment remains only partially satisfied and there is due and owing as of this date principal and interest in the amount of $4,239,84. Interest accrues at the rate of $1.06 per day.

Would you please advise whether or not you would be interested in collecting on this judgment and, if so, your fees for doing so. It's entirely possible that a letter from you to Mr. Broomell will be all that's needed.

On August 8, 1988, Steven Corris responded:

Dear Ms. Klempt:

    I apologize for not getting back to you sooner, but I have been in and out of the office for the past six weeks. Seems that there's never enough time. I want to thank you for offering me the opportunity to collect the judgment on behalf of Ms. Broomell, but I must decline.

    Without sounding pretentious, my current retainer for cases is a flat $100,000, with an additional charge of $1,000 per hour. Since I specialize in international trade and geopolitical relations between the Middle East and Europe, my clientele is very unique and limited, and I am afraid I am unable to accept other work at this time.

    I am enclosing the copy of the judgment you sent me and again, Ms. Klempt, I thank you for your thoughts. It was very nice of you.

On August 17, 1988, Becky Klempt wrote Steve Curris a second letter. Sort of a thank-you for his no-thank-you:

Dear Steve:

    I am in receipt of your letter....Steve, I've got news for you—you can't say you charge a $100,000 retainer fee and an additional $1,000 an hour without sounding pretentious. It just can't be done. Especially when you're writing to someone in Laramie, Wyoming, where you're considered

pretentious if you wear socks to court or drive anything fancier than a Ford Bronco. Hell, Steve, all the lawyers in Laramie put together don't charge $1,000 an hour.

Anyway, we were sitting around the office discussing your letter and decided that you had a good thing going. We doubt we could get away with charging $1,000 an hour in Laramie (where people are more inclined to barter livestock than pay in cash), but we do believe we could join you in California, where evidently people can get away with just about anything. Therefore, the four lawyers in our firm intend to join you in the practice of international trade and geopolitical relations between the Middle East and Europe.

Now, Steve, you're probably thinking that we don't know anything about the Middle East and Europe, but I think you'll be pleasantly surprised to find that this is not the case. Paul Schierer is actually from the Middle East—he was raised outside Chicago, and although those national newsmen insist on calling Illinois the Midwest, to us, if it's between New York and the Missouri River, it's the Middle East.

Additionally, although I have never personally been to Europe, my sister just returned from a vacation there and told me lots about it, so I believe I would be of some help to you on that end of the negotiations. Hoke MacMillan has actually been there, although it was 15 years ago, so you might have to update him on recent geopolitical developments. Also, Hoke has applied to the Rotary Foreign Exchange Program for a 16 year old Swedish girl and believes she will be helpful in preparing him for trips abroad.

Another thing you should know, Steve, is that the firm has an extensive foreign language background, which I believe would be useful to you. Hoke took Latin in high school, although he hasn't used it much as he did not become a pharmacist or a priest. Vonnie Nagel took high school German, while Paul has eaten in Italian restaurants. I, myself, majored in French in college, until I realized that probably wasn't the smartest career move in the world. I've forgotten such words as "international" and "geopolitical" (which I'm not too familiar with in English), but I can still hail a taxi or find a restroom, which might come in handy.

Steve, let us know when we should join you in California so that we can begin doing whatever it is you do. In anticipation of our move, we've all been practicing trying to say we charge $1,000 an hour with a straight face, but so far we haven't been able to do it. I suspect it'll be easier once we actually reach California where I understand they charge $5,000,000 for one-bedroom condos and everybody (even poor people) drive Mercedes. Anyway, because I'll be new to the area of international trade and geopolitical relations, I'm thinking of only charging $500-600 an hour to begin with. Will that be enough to meet our overhead?

I look forward to hearing from you before you go away again for six weeks....

P.S. Incidentally, we have advised our client of your hourly rate. She is willing to pay you $1,000 per hour to collect this judgment, provided it doesn't take you more than four seconds.

Becky received worldwide publicity when folks began to leak her letter to the news media ("a lawyer with a sense of humor!"). Not to mention a marriage proposal from at least one stranger.

*****

And then there's Phoenix, Arizona's Mick LaValle. Mick got ticked by the pleading tactics of a lawyer on the other side of the *v.* in a case he was handling. Evidently the urge to explode welled up inside him and found an outlet in a letter to this person, with some suggestions for continuing professional education:[59]

Dear Mr. Smythe:

I have your second Motion to Compel, one filed after you had received our 458 pages of answers to your 137 Interrogatories. Ms. Chones, who churns out this paperwork for you, and you, as her supervisor, need to try *chilla makusa.*[60]

In the East Indian Sufi religion, *"chilla"* means a retreat of 40 days duration with fasting, prayer, and recollection, based on the 40-day fast of Moses, when, as the Koran says, he received a vision of God. *"Chilla makusa"* is a little bit more elaborate. It requires the candidate to hang upside down in a well, while engaged in prescribed prayers and meditation, using the procedure known as *dhikr*, the constant repetition of a sacred word or

---

[59]To protect the culpable, names are changed in this letter, which was printed previously in Judge Jerry Buchmeyer's "et cetera" column in *Dallas Bar Association Headnotes* (10-15-90).

[60][Author's, as opposed to letter-writer's, note:] Not to be confused with *akuna matada*, the "No Worries" phrase made famous by Disney's *The Lion King*.

phrase, aloud or silent, hundreds of times a day—e.g., "There is no God but God." *I suggest that Ms. Chones' dhikr should be, "It is wrong to churn fees," and yours should be, "Litigators should try cases."*

In *chilla makusa*, the candidate is finally brought into the convent, the *tauhid-khana* (the house of unity), and there he faces Mecca, sitting on the carpet on his knees, his heels under his buttocks (the position known in the Islamic world as *"jalsa"*). He then proceeds into a long series or prayers, private meditations, readings from the Koran on God's holy mercy and the prophets, absorbing homilies and exhortations, slowly evolving into *tariga*, the mystical path of the Sufi brotherhood, producing a profound transformation that infuses one's thinking for the rest of his life and which can never be shaken off.

All this would result in disputes that actually went to trial, forests that grow taller and greener, and associates who develop abilities actually related to the meaningful practice of law. Try it.

Mick and I are on the same wavelength in this regard. My mother hasn't a clue about motions to compel, interrogatories, and the like.

Very few, if any, of Perry Mason's letters were ever read on the TV show. And the Dream Team's correspondence file is sealed—until the right offer comes along.

15

MR. BEAUDOIN V. MR. RAJNEESH

Why shouldn't truth be stranger than fiction?
Fiction, after all, has to make sense.
—Mark Twain

"Ye shall know the truth, and the truth shall set you free." Or something like that.

Once again I remind the reader (or reader*s*, I hope) that I engage in no fiction whatever. Nor do I repeat lawyer jokes.[61]

Moreso than others, lawyers find themselves (physically, not psychologically) in the presence of people who have taken "THE OATH." Other than dealing with the Shakespearian urge some people have to bring about their demise, perhaps the most trying and tribulational aspect of being RAs is the inevitability of being frequently in the presence of people who have sworn to tell the Truth.

Volumes have been written about the importance of THE OATH which witnesses take before testifying in court

---

[61]Although, in weak moments, I occasionally turn them into reporter jokes or insurance agent jokes.

or at a deposition. While it may vary a bit from jurisdiction to jurisdiction, THE OATH basically goes[62] like this:

"Do you solemnly swear or affirm that the testimony you are about to give will be the truth, the whole truth, and nothing but the truth, so help you God?"

"I do."[63]

Once THE OATH is administered, lawyers and witnesses engage in the strangest dialogue. I offer evidence of this fact. Consider the cross-examination of Mr. Beaudoin, an expert in a plane crash case. It was claimed that the pilot should have been warned of bad weather seen earlier by *six* FAA employees:

Q. ...I am going to read to you a poem called "The Blind Men and the Elephant"...by John Godfrey Saxe:

---

[62]I think this is a correct usage of the verb "to go." Remember this usage: "I know a dance and it *goes like* this..."? I think, but cannot be certain, that this usage was the precursor to the slang of today, in which people (mostly kids?) use the verb "to go" and the adjective "like" interchangeably to mean "say" or "think." *E.g.*,

"She goes, 'Where did you get that dress?' And I go, 'It's none of your business!' And then she's like, 'Who do you think you are, talking to me like that?' And I'm like, 'Will you please get out of my face?'"

[63]However, it must be noted that when one's religious beliefs conflict with the oath, substitute oaths, consistent with the witness's religion are acceptable.

It was six men of Indostan
        To learning much inclined,
Who went to see the Elephant
        (Though all of them were blind),
That each by observation
        Might satisfy his mind.

The First approached the elephant,
        And happening to fall
Against his broad and sturdy side,
        At once began to bawl:
"God bless me! but the Elephant
        Is very like a wall!"

The Second, feeling of the tusk,
        Cried, "Ho! what have we here
So very round and smooth and sharp?
        To me 'tis mighty clear
This wonder of an Elephant
        Is very like a spear!"

(I assure you—I am not making this up.)

The Third approached the animal,
        And happening to take
The squirming trunk within his hands,
        Thus boldly up and spake:
"I see," quoth he, "the Elephant
        Is very like a snake!"

The Fourth reached out an eager hand,
And felt about the knee.
"What this most wondrous beast is like
Is mighty plain," quoth he;
"'Tis clear enough the Elephant
Is very like a tree!"

The Fifth, who chanced to touch the ear,
Said: "E'en the blindest man
Can tell what this resembles most;
Deny the fact who can,
This marvel of an Elephant
Is very like a fan!"

The Sixth no sooner had begun
About the beast to grope,
Than seizing on the swinging tail
That fell within his scope,
"I see," quoth he, "the Elephant
Is very like a rope!"

And so these men of Indostan
Disputed loud and long,
Each in his own opinion
Exceeding stiff and strong,
Though each was partly in the right
And all were in the wrong!

Q. ...Mr. Beaudoin,...would you not agree that those six men in that tower who did not see the hazardous [weather] condition were mighty like the six blind men of Indostan?...

A. Obviously, I wouldn't agree....[M]aybe the blind men were in the cockpit because they saw lightning, they saw weather, and they continued their approach.

Q. ...I'd like to ask you to substitute an elephant for the thunderstorm for the purpose of this question. Is it not true that if a reasonably prudent controller saw an elephant right north of the runway, the controller would not say, "I see an elephant, [but rather] I see what appears to be a fan or a snake and so forth"?...

A. Sir, we don't cover elephants in our handbook. We talk about elements of weather. We would pass on the elements that we observe [such as lightning, rain, or a thunderstorm] to a pilot and then the pilot can determine whether or not it's an elephant....

(At least one reader has by now attacked my credibility, arguing that since I am not under oath, the foregoing is obviously a hoax. Not so. It is true courtroom dialogue from an actual case. It continues:)

Q. Do you agree...that heavy rain is more hazardous to flight navigation than light rain?

A. I wouldn't agree with that....Heavy rain is not a detriment to flight.

Q. Would you agree that a thunderstorm is more hazardous to flight navigation than light rain?...

A. [G]enerally a thunderstorm could be more hazardous than any rain....

Q. Based on what you know, is it your opinion that [the pilot] was of the opinion that he was in light rain when he reported the rain to the controller?

A. That's very difficult to answer because he says he's "in the rain, feels good." To me, that means he is

*encountering rain of some intensity and...not encountering
any turbulence....*

*Q. I'm going to ask you a hypothetical question,
Mr. Beaudoin....I am going to ask you to assume that you
are a pretty good tap dancer....I'm going to ask you to
assume that you enjoy tap dancing. Now, assuming those
two facts, would you rather tap dance with Gene Kelly in
a light rain or in a thunderstorm?*

A. Am I inside a building?

Q. No, you're outside.

A. That's my only choice? Gene Kelly?

Q. Yes, sir.

*A. [There are] other people I'd rather tap dance
with.*

(For some strange reason, I feel again impelled to
remind you: I am not making this up.) The lawyer
continued:

*Q. Well, I'm asking you to assume that your most
favorite person to tap dance with would be Gene
Kelly....Would you rather tap dance with Gene Kelly in the
light rain or in the thunderstorm?*

*A. I probably would like light rain. We could go
with "Singing in the Rain" and dancing in the rain, things
like that.*

Q. Because it would feel good, wouldn't it?

*A. Probably wouldn't feel too good if it's raining on
you....I wouldn't want to tap dance in the rain, period! But
if I had to pick light rain rather than heavy rain, I guess I
would pick light.*

When the cross-examiner was finally through, the judge commented that he was certain the lawyer would see his name in the paper the following day.[64]

*****

Inasmuch as an earlier footnote in this chapter advised the reader that religious beliefs were accommodatable by the Oath, I must not fail to mention and set forth the following excerpt from the deposition of Bhagwan Shree Rajneesh:[65]

Lawyer. Would you swear the witness, please.

Clerk. Yes. I take an oath on the sacred book of Rajneeshism that I only speak the truth and will only speak the truth now, under pain and penalties of perjury.

Witness. Your Honor, before I take the oath, I have to say a few things. Otherwise, the oath will be a fraud. The first thing, I have always been against the ritual of oath-taking, for the simple reason that if a man is capable of lying, he can lie even while he is taking an oath. His oath can be a lie. And if a man is a man of truth, the oath creates a dilemma for that man. For the man of truth to take an oath means that he is capable of lying—without the oath he will lie, and with the oath he will say the truth....[B]ut I will take this oath, just to play the game of this deposition. I will follow the rule. But, I would like you

---

[64]All as reported in Buchmeyer, "et cetera," *Texas Bar Journal* (Oct. 1988), referring to "the Delta 191 trial" then pending in federal court and being tried in Fort Worth, Texas.

[65]As reported in the Idaho State Bar magazine, *The Advocate* (April 1992).

to remember that by taking the oath, I am lying in the first place. It is against my philosophy of life, and you are forcing me to take the oath. That means you are freeing me; giving me the freedom to lie later on, although I am not going to lie. But, in spite of that freedom, I will only say the truth because I am incapable of lying. That is impossible. That is against my being and my existence. Now, just to play the game, I will take the oath. You can repeat what you want.

Following which statement to His or Her Honor, the witness was then and there oathified, observing verbally in the process that "this is such ridiculousness that I am taking an oath on my own words."

****

I don't recall any disputes about THE OATH as such in the O.J. case. But now that the oath has been properly introduced in these pages, let's move right along and witness some more....

16

LAY WITNESSES ON MEDICAL MATTERS

The art of medicine consists of amusing the patient while nature cures the disease.
—Voltaire

Moving right along, let us recall that the point on which I am offering proof is that once THE OATH is administered, the dialogue that follows is often quite strange. Recall also that none of this is made-up stuff. It is Truth, with a capital *T*.

Non-medical people under oath, referred to for some strange reason as "lay witnesses," have a curious approach to the Truth when the topic at hand has to do with medical matters. Consider this good faith effort to ensure that the lawyer fully understood the diagnosis:

Q. Could you tell how bad his legs were torn up?

A. Bad. Real bad.

Q. Describe, if you can recall, what they looked like.

A. Have you ever seen a cow butchered with a chain saw?

For some reason lawyers seldom answer witnesses when such questions are put forth.

*****

But here is one in which the lawyer (a male) did answer the question put to him by the witness (a female) or at least he may be said to have attempted to answer:

Q. Let's break down the different problems that you're having. The shoulder pain itself—can you give me any words to describe what that feels like?

A. Have you ever worn a bra that was too tight on you?

Q. If I said yes, my mother would be very astonished. No, I can't say that I have.

Now, here's a guy who's got the same mother-problem that I exhibited earlier in the text.

*****

In the following instance, the medical condition of pregnancy was at issue. The witness was not a happy father:

Q. In connection with the plaintiff's pregnancy, in what way do you believe that she "cheated" you?

A. I feel like she cheated me because she said she couldn't get pregnant because she had an operation for cancer of the uterine or astigmatism or something like that.

Perhaps the couple in question just did not see eye to eye.

*****

This is from a workers' compensation hearing. The primary issue had been a sore back, the alleged result of a fall on the job. The claimant testified that she had had breast reduction surgery. The cross-examiner inquired further:

Q. Did the size of your breasts have any relation to your back pain?

A. I did not have the pain before the fall, but I did have the breasts.[66]

I guess she told him.

*****

And speaking of pain and suffering, not to mention giving equal time to the other gender:

Q. When did you first experience pain after the accident?

A. Immediately. I was bruised and skinned pretty good, and my right tentacle had swollen to the size of a hard baseball.

THE RECORD is silent as to the condition of the other seven tentacles.

*****

---

[66]*Fields v. Travelers Ins. Co.*, Harrison County, Texas, District Ct. No. 40,231.

Idiomatic questions are often ill-advised when the witness is in the least bit perturbed. The attorney should have seen this one coming, probably:

> *Q. Are you seeing anybody, an ear specialist?*
> *A. I saw one about a month and a half ago.*
> *Q. Who was that?*
> *A. Dr. Ripp....R-I-P-P.*
> *Q. Does he have a first name?*
> *A. Probably.*

I wonder if that's with two <u>b's</u> or three?

*****

And then sometimes the good faith with which the witness answers the casual query just sort of jumps out at you:

> *Q. [When] was the last time you saw Dr. Bryant?*
> *A. 1953...*
> *Q. What kind of things did he treat you for?*
> *A. Tonsillitis and acute nosebleed.*
> *Q. What caused the nosebleed?*
> *A. I don't know, but it was a booger.*

Have I assured you lately that I am not making this up?

*****

I'll let you judge for yourself the mental state of the witness in this next example:

Q. Has there ever been a time in your life where you've considered yourself to have a drinking problem?

A. I really never considered it a problem. It was about the easiest thing I ever done.

Now, that's what I call candor, with a non-capital *c*.

*****

The following is from the deposition of a worker who was badly injured in an incident in which he was aloft in a "cherry picker," or man lift, and he "accidentally touched the wire that [he] didn't want to touch" because "the saw slipped":

Q. When the saw came into contact with the wire,...what happened to you?...

A. It froze me up there....I wasn't able to do anything.

Q.....Do you know what happened next?

A. Well, all I can tell you is what they told me.

Q. Okay. That's fair enough. Tell me who it is that had told you.

A. Mr. Sistruck, the gentleman that was there with me.

Q. Okay. What has he told you?

A. He told me that...when the electricity hit me, it froze me up there. He in turn ran over to the machine....He hit the down button....and it pulled me down, it let the man lift down, which pulled me away from the wire. They drug me out of the bucket. And by that time, I guess several people came out, and somebody called the paramedics. And once Mr. Sistruck got me out of the bucket, he gave me artificial insemination—you know, mouth to mouth.... [67]

*****

The following is from a deposition of an auto accident victim:

Q. Did you stay in the car until the ambulance arrived?

A. Yes, I did.

Q. Did the ambulance attendants help you out of the car?

A. They were going to put me on a backboard and put a neck brace on, and I told them I would prefer to walk to the ambulance.

---

[67]*Amy v. Emmpco*, Cuyahoga County, Ohio, Ct. of Common Pleas, No. 132,142. I called one of the firms involved in the case and requested a copy of an excerpt of the deposition. I received it a few days later, but in the interim I received a copy of an intra-firm

MEMORANDUM

June 5, 1990

TO: Mr. McGinnis
FROM: Mr. Eilers

RE: Artificial Insemination

Your cross-examination several years ago of Hardy Amy continues to provoke inquiries from disbelieving counsel around the country and to otherwise distract me from proper handling of current matters. Since it was you who coerced Mr. Amy into conceding that he was given oral "artificial insemination," I ask that you respond to Mr. Fleming's request....

A. They were going to put me on a backboard and put a neck brace on, and I told them I would prefer to walk to the ambulance.

Q. ....[W]hy did you volunteer to walk to the ambulance rather than have them carry you over there?

A. Have you ever been on a backboard?

Q. I can't honestly say that I know—

A. They're not very comfortable. And I was—my back hurt anyway....And I did not want to lie on a backboard.

Q. When were you on a backboard before?

A. I used to date an ambulance driver.

Q. Should I ask—

A. What I was doing on the backboard?

Mr. Patillo: We may need to go off the record for just a minute.

Witness: It's not what you think.

Q. Well, if it's not what I think, why were you on the backboard?

A. Just because I wanted to lie on the backboard—just to see what it felt like.

THE RECORD (mine, anyway) contains no elaboration as to what it does feel like to lie on such a backboard.

17

MORE THAN A RECORD

Judge a man by his questions rather than by his answers.
—Voltaire

Sometimes it may seem that the RAs (previously referred to as "Real Attorneys") who ask the questions are themselves affected by THE OATH. For example:

Q. What else did they take X-rays of—other than your knees, or your heads?

A. Heads?

Q. Your head. In fact, you only have one head, correct?

And, for another example:

Q. Now, Mrs. James, no other child was born to or adopted by the deceased?

A. No.

Q. And no child is expected?

And another:

Q. How long have you lived on this land?

A. All my life.

Q. And where did you live before then?

And yet one more example (before the onset of the asterisks):

Q. What is the nature of your relationship to Johnny Darrell Bailey?

A. I'm his mother.

Q. And you have been all his life?

Okay, if you insist, one more preliminary example (a spicy one):

Q. Do you recall the first time that you had sexual relations with Mrs. Johnson?

A. If you are looking for an exact date, no....

Q. Do you recall how many times?

A. Probably six times, I guess, within a six-month period....

Q. Where did you have sexual relations with her? Where was the physical location?

A. In my pickup.

Q. In your pickup?

A. Yes.

Q. And that was the only place?

A. Yes.

Q. And was that parked? Were you parked?....

Those are real questions. Really asked by RAs to real witnesses.

*****

Attorneys sometimes ask unnecessary questions, for purposes of THE RECORD. Knowing that a transcription of testimony may, at some point in the future, be important for purpose of an appeal, the lawyer may tend to inject *legalities* into questions. *E.g.,* "And was the payment of a thousand dollars the bargained for consideration in this contract?"[68]

And another example, less legalistic, from the deposition of the plaintiff in a personal injury case involving pain (male lawyer, female witness):

Q. And the tenderness would be down below the belt?

A. Yes.

Q. In the upper part of the buttocks?

A. In and around that area.

Mr. Howie: Is it the part you sit on or the vertical part?

A. I guess the vertical part, but not totally underneath.

Q. Okay. So, as you are sitting in a chair, you would be able to put your hand on it without sliding your hand under your hip?

A. But it doesn't feel so from the outside, you know.

Mr. Howie: But we're just trying to figure out where it is located. We're not trying to feel it.

A. You better not!

Q. I know that. For the record, I am a good 18 inches or two feet away from you, Susan.

*****

---

[68]This is a leading question, the likes of which are usually taboo. Also, it calls, in some degree, for a legal conclusion, which is also taboo to a certain extent. Usually such a question will follow factual and simple questioning that has established that the witness paid $1,000 for whatever object was involved.

But there are times when you just gotta wonder what was on the mind of the inquisitor. If anything. Consider the following:

Q. When was your son born?
A. 1956.
Q. Was this before or after your hysterectomy?

Maybe the lawyer was hoping to make medico-legal history with that witness. And that question.

*****

Reading this next one, you can feel a sense of surprise overwhelm the lawyer. Who then cannot resist asking one question too many (sometimes possibly referred to later as "OQTM"[69]):

Q. Now, I'm going to show you what has been marked as State's Exhibit No. 2 and ask if you recognize this picture?
A. John Fletcher.
Q. That's you?
A. Yes sir.

---

[69]The classic OQTM, taught to every law student, involves a fight in which the defendant is alleged to have bitten off the plaintiff's nose. On cross-examination an eye witness says he did not actually *see* the defendant bite the plaintiff's nose off. The OQTM, asked by defense counsel, is, "If you didn't see him bite the plaintiff's nose off, then how can you know it happened?" To which the answer was, "Well, I saw him spit it out."

Q. And you were present when the picture was taken, right?

And when the lawyer later read that part of the deposition, he was not completely certain that he himself had been present when he took the witness's deposition.

*****

You decide whether this is a case of one too many questions or a case of one too many answers:

Q. You've determined that...to compensate Mr. White for the present value of his future loss of projected earning capacity, Mr. White would have to be paid approximately $123,000 in cash today, true?

Y. Yes.

Q. Now, if the tooth fairy flitted into the room and increased that number by 25 percent and sprinkled an additional $35,000 on Mr. White as an additional compensation for the present value of his projected lost earning capacity, then according to your model and your calculations, that additional $35,000 would be overcompensation to Mr. White, wouldn't it?

*A. If the tooth fairy gave him an extra $35,000...,
then that would certainly make him re-evaluate his belief in the tooth fairy.*

"BOW-PING!" I think I heard the claimant's lawyer say!

*****

The lawyer who engaged in the following dialogue admitted a bit of frustration as he questioned a supposed

expert in a truck brake failure case, the witness having testified that he had no prior professional experience in evaluating brake failures on trucks:

Q. I mean, what you're telling me, Mr. McAninch, is that if I walk into your office and say, "Mr. McAninch, my knee hurts and the joint in my knee hurts," and you're a professional engineer, you feel comfortable in operating on my knee. Is that what you're telling me?

A. No. Engineers shoot lawyers with bad knees.

Apparently a good sport, the lawyer responded, on THE RECORD, "I see. All right. Well taken, well taken."

*****

To what extent the following illustration contained anything that was well-taken, I will let you judge:

Q. Now. Mrs. Deering, were you the daughter of [the late] W.T. "Hooker" Vandergrift, as we all knew him?

A. Yes. I was.

Q. In what capacity?

A. Well, he sired me.

*****

Before we get completely off the subject of siring, here's another clever question formulated by a legally trained mind:

Q. ...Can you tell us where you were born?

A. Memphis.

Q. Memphis, Texas?

A. Yes, sir.

Q. And when was that?

A. August 20, 1953.

Q. ...Did you live in Memphis, or did you move somewhere? Or did you just go there to be born...?

*****

The following is thought to be rather self-explanatory ("RSE"):

Q. Do you find—do you know cows at all?

A. I've never known one personally.

Q. Do you associate with cows?

A. I've been around cows.

Q. Are they smart animals? Do you know them to be smart animals?

A. Well, let's see. Having never known one personally but having worked on a farm as a child, they know when it's time to come to the barn. They know where to go.

Q. Outside of meat and milk and manure, they're fairly useless animals, are they not?

A. Oh, I don't think someone in the dairy business would say that. I think that—

Q. Outside of the meat, milk, and manure, the three M's, okay?

A. The three big M's.

I know of no litigation having been threatened by Minnesota, Mining & Manufacturing Co. as a result of this exchange.

*****

The flow of a deposition is sometimes such that one asks a question to which the answer is rather obvious:

Q. Did you hurt yourself while working for Hensle-Phelps Construction Co.?

A. Yes.

Q. And what happened?

A. Got bit by a bobcat....

Q. I take it that is a wild animal?

A. It was when I found it.

*****

In the next illustration the lawyer may have been having a problem with conceiving the concept of conception:

Q. Do you know how far pregnant you are right now?

A. I will be three months on November 8th.

Q. Apparently then, the date of conception was August 8th?

A. Yes.

Q. What were you and your husband doing at that time?

(What the hell did he think they were doing?)

*****

I cannot conceive how THE RECORD was enhanced in any of the just recited instances. Which distinguishes them from the following, in which the *unavailability* of a witness was obviously an important legality[70] which the lawyer wanted in THE RECORD:

> *Q. And you testified that Cecil Melis is now dead?*
> *A. That's correct.*
> *Q. Do you recall when he died?*
> *A. Very recently. This year: March, April, May. I do not recall the date.*
> *Q. Okay. So he's not available to testify in this hearing..., is that right?*

We rather hope so, anyway.

*****

And, possibly at least, in the following example, the *audibility* of what the witness had been told could possibly have become an issue the attorney needed to be in THE RECORD:

> *A. He told me he was seeking a major insurance policy...to protect [against] a catastrophe or an untimely death to himself, and he wanted to have the funds available to perpetuate the company.*
> *Q. Did he want [the company] to pass to his children?*
> *A. No, [he wanted me to have it].*
> *Q. And when did he tell you that, Steve?*

---

[70]Without going into great detail (meaning I'm not opening a book for purposes of writing this Clever Footnote), when a witness is *unavailable*, certain evidentiary items may be used that otherwise are precluded from use—e.g., the witness's deposition.

A. He told me that numerous times.

Q. Prior to his death?

Whereupon, one of the other lawyers present piped up and said, "No. *After* his death."

*****

Perhaps it is something about the topic of death that causes lawyers' minds to wander off. The lawyer in the following example was, I believe, attempting to be quite sensitive in his handling of a potentially emotional issue, of which death was a component. But his mind wandered off:

Q. Mrs. Smith, do you believe that you are emotionally unstable?

A. I used to be.

Q. How many times have you committed suicide?

Assuring you once again that I do not make up any of these things,...

*****

...I offer another example of how the sensitive nature of death seemed to cause a lawyer to ask—well, a stupid question:

Q. Now, Mrs. Johnson, how was your first marriage terminated?

A. By death.

Q. And by whose death was it terminated?

*****

And yet another:

Q. How long did Dr. Payne treat you or see you or take care of your family?

A. Since I was about eight years old.

Q. Until when you left.

A. Yes, sir. He still sees me today.

Q. Okay. So he's your doctor again?

A. Yes, sir.

Q. I take it he's living, then?

To which the witness correctly replied in the affirmative.

*****

Okay, one more on how the topic of death evokes mindless questions:

Q. When did you last see Walter?

A. At his funeral.

Q. Did he make any comment to you at that time?

*****

But here's an illustration of how the concept of death did not confuse things at all:

Q. Did you ever have any conversations with Jill about this $16,000 check?

A. Oh, yeah. Well, let's put it this way: I had limited access to Jill after she died. Her attorney kept her out of the meetings.

Jill was probably off with Bernie during those meetings, making movies.

*****

And another example where death was no obstacle (to a CPA witness, who had forecast some economic situations):

Q. And was that also based on the fact that the plaintiff told you he wouldn't quit before 55?

A....That's correct. I don't know what else I could have based it on, except he indicated he would not have terminated his employment prior to early retirement age. And, of course, now, if he would have died during that period of time, he probably would have had to terminate his employment because he wouldn't have had any other alternative.

An astute observation. And sound reasoning.

*****

Pregnancy is a medical condition that tends to confuse the most educated of lawyers:

Q. And, Doctor, as a result of your examination of the plaintiff in this case, was the young lady pregnant?

A. The young lady was pregnant, but not as a result of my examination.

Bad question, good answer.

*****

Compare the preceding to the following bad answer, bad question exchange:

Q. When was the last time she was employed?

A. Several months ago. She's expecting at this time.

Q. Okay. A child?
A. Yes, sir. I think that's what it is.
Let's hope.

*****

When witnesses give short affirmative and negative answers to questions, it is difficult when reading the exchanges to know what the lawyer is thinking. But in the following exchange the lawyer's admiration of the witness is made clear at the end—by his question:

Q. Do you have your own checking account?
A. No, I don't.
Q. Do you write checks?
A. Yes.
Q. Do you have a joint account?
A. Yes.
Q. Do you know how much is in that joint account?
A. No, I don't.
Q. Do you know how much money your husband makes?
A. No, I don't.
Q. Do you know what the name of your husband's company is?
A. No, I don't.
Q. Do you know how long your husband has been self-employed?
A. No, I don't know how long.
Q. How do you know if there is money in your checking account at the time you write a check?
A. My husband tells me.

Q. Do you ask your husband's permission before you write any checks?
A. Yes, I do.
Q. Will you marry me?

The witness's answer to the question was not reported, and the court reporter's reaction to the question necessitated a break in the deposition.

*****

There is more. Like this unintentional poetic exchange ("UPE"):
Q. Who else?
A. A man named Clyde Dodd.
Q. Dodd?
A. Yeah. He's dead.
Q. Dead?
A. Very dead.
Mr. C.: He died? Dodd?
A. Clyde died.
Mr. R.: In degrees of death, he's at the extreme?[71]
A. Yes....
Q. What was he, a bookie or a friend?

(Read that one over again—aloud this time, with a friend, and try to keep from laughing.)

*****

---

[71]What a question, huh? Let's hear it for this guy!

And, finally (for this chapter, that is), there is this classic excerpt from the deposition of a pathologist:

> *Q. Do you recognize the person in Plaintiff's Exhibit 8?*
> *A. Yes....It is Mr. Edgington.*
> *Q. Do you recall the time that you examined the body of Mr. Edgington at the Rose Chapel?*
> *A. It was in the evening. The autopsy started at about 8:30 p.m.*
> *Q. And Mr. Edgington was dead at that time, is that correct?*

Whereupon, and being still under oath, the pathologist testified, *"No, you dumb asshole. He was sitting there on the table wondering why I was doing an autopsy!"*

Without question, a chapter ender.

(And, yes, this would be among the *long* chapters my mother had in mind when she insisted I write this book.)

18

CANINE CREDIBILITY *V.*
COMATOSE CONCEPTION

Quite literally, a man's memory is what he forgets with.
—Odell Shepard

With this chapter I shall began to ease into the Memory Thing (possibly referred to hereinafter, if at all, as the "MT," not to be confused with the word that is pronounced when those letters are said aloud). An important precept of the MT is that if you don't remember something, it is practically impossible to discuss it with any degree of intelligence—unless you are under oath.

The following medico-legal discussion is from the transcript of a paternity trial. The defendant/witness (who, like one of the earlier cited deponents, was not a happy father) was a retired law professor. The plaintiff was a former client of his who, in order to pay her legal fee, had performed certain maid-type services. The defendant adamantly denied ever having had a relationship with the plaintiff, but (being possessed of a legally trained mind) he could not resolutely deny the *possibility* that the child might be his.

In contrast to the preceding chapter's examples, the following offers some brilliant questions by counsel. See if you can pick them out without my help:

Q. How is it possible that you could be the father of this child without having had sexual contact with Maryann?

A. There are a number of ways. One is artificial insemination.

Q. Did that happen in this case?

A. I don't know.

Q. Are you a donor at a sperm bank here in town?

A. No, I'm not a donor.

Q. Okay. How would Maryann artificially inseminate herself with your sperm?

A. I'm not quite certain that it did occur, but there was a possibility of it occurring.

Q. How would she get ahold of your sperm?

A. She cleaned my office from time to time...and there was some refrigerated sperm in the refrigerator during that...period of time.

Q. And so your theory...is that Maryann got into your refrigerator and inseminated herself with your sperm? That's your testimony?

DEFENSE COUNSEL: Object to counsel's manner of asking the question—[he's] laughing.

(For educational reasons I interrupt the testimony at this juncture to point out that neither the rules of civil procedure nor the rules of evidence forbid laughter in the courtroom; but the opposing lawyer felt it necessary to get on THE RECORD the fact that the questioning lawyer was being derisive. And I reiterate: I am not making this up.) Read on:

Q. I'm trying not to be facetious. Is that your theory?

A. I don't have any theory. You're asking me how it's possible and that's what I told you, among other things. I don't know.

Q. What would the other things be?

A. I told you I don't recall having any...sexual contact with Maryann and that's the truth. I don't have any recollection of it. If this could happen at a time when I was comatose, that's a possibility.

Q. Were you comatose in February or March of 1985?[72]

A. There was a period of time when I was under very heavy sedation for what has never been truly diagnosed, but something that kept me from being able to walk.

Q. And you were sedated and Maryann had access to your body? So that's a possibility? She may have...raped you without your knowledge? Is that what you're telling us?

A. I don't know if you want a technical definition of rape. I'm guessing. If, in fact, the child is mine, that's another way it could have happened.

Let's just say it was a litigious conception and leave it at that for now.

*****

But so that the easing into the MT will not be so stressful, let us now examine a case in which the human memories all seemed to be working well, although contradictory to each other.

---

[72]If you picked this as one of the brilliant questions, you win!

DOG HITS CAR, CAR OWNER SUCCESSFUL
IN DAMAGE SUIT. That might have been the headline for
the next illustration. In Fayetteville, Arkansas, Mr. and
Mrs. Bolstad had parked their car in the lot of the VA
Hospital and had gone in to fill out some paperwork
pertaining to Mr. Bolstad's medical retirement. They left
their dog, P.J., "a tiny Boston Terrier," in the car with all
the windows down.

When Mrs. Bolstad came out to check on P.J.
several minutes later, a guard came up to her and told her
that P.J. "has hit a car" and "you need to come around
front with me." Obviously, the car owner ultimately filed
suit—in small claims court—and won a $312 judgment. The
Bolstads appealed to circuit court, where, during the trial,
Mr. Bolstad testified as follows:

*Q. [T]ell me in your own words[73] what happened
the day that all these events supposedly took place.*

*A. [T]he wife and I, Nancy,...parked on the south
side of the building..., and I had all four windows
down....The dog was in the car, and I went into
Personnel....I was inside about twenty minutes. At the ten
minute mark the wife went back out to check on the dog,
and he was in the car at that time. She came back in [and]
there was seven, eight minutes more involved there. We
went back out to the car, and the dog was in the car. He
was sitting on the little arm rest between the two front*

---

[73]This phrase crops up a lot—"in your own words." Who
else's words does one think a witness is going to use? What do
they think the witness might say? "Oh, according to Dan Rather
on the CBS Evening News, I was walking along Main Street...."

seats....Bobby, the guard, came running between the two buildings, and he said, "Your dog hit a car up front."

(Once more I swear and affirm: I am not making this up.) This man's testimony continues:

A. The dog's in the car. He looks good to me..., but we drove around the building and pulled up behind her little red car, and I wanted the dog to tell me what happened. So, I let the dog out with me....I took the dog over by the car. He showed no ill feelings or anything. Then I was concerned...about the dog...because if he made a dent that size and creased it until it actually had metal protruding, he had to be hurt, and if he hit that mirror, there was no doubt in my mind that he was hurt internally....I brought the dog out for two reasons. One is to see what his attitude toward the car was, and also to have the guard and I check him for injuries."

Mr. Bolstad hammered home his point by saying that, while P.J.—"no bigger than my nine month old grandson"—had previously gotten out of the car by jumping out the window, he had never been known to be able to get back in by that method. And then the wife's testimony was presented. And, possibly, as one might expect of a woman who allows herself to be referred to as "the wife," the questions were more leading in nature:

Q. You left the dog in the car?

A. Uh-huh.

Q. Have you ever had any problems with the dog getting out of the car or leaving or going where it's not supposed to?

A. No....[74]

Q. Now, when you took the dog out to the car, did he show any remorse?

A. No.

Q. And he acts real guilty about anything he does?

A. Oh, yeah.[75]

The judgment against P.J. was affirmed—all $312 of it. And, unlike Little Thunder Jim and the Mississippi suck-egg dogs, P.J. lived to tell his tale. But the court didn't believe him.

THE CRUCIAL ISSUE, LADIES AND GENTLEMEN, IS THE TERRIER'S CREDIBILITY: DID P.J. SHOW REMORSE? OR DID HE NOT?

---

[74]Fast forward through the cumulative part about going into the Personnel Office, etc.

[75]*Bolstad v. Perguson*, Washington County, Arkansas, Circuit No. Civ 90-0284; Arkansas Supreme Court No. 90-361.

19

THE MOUTHS OF BABES

In every real man is hidden a child who wants to play.
—Friedrich Nietzsche

My extensive study of sworn testimony leads me also to believe that once THE OATH is administered, some witnesses, in the best of faith, give the strangest of answers. This is especially true of children. Art Linkletter was right on when he observed that *Kids Say the Darnedest Things*. They do— especially when they are under oath.

The oath is usually administered in a special way for children, as the court must ensure that THE RECORD reflects that the child really and truly understands. You probably remember the scene from *Miracle on Thirty-Fourth Street*, where the prosecutor's son takes the stand, and the judge asks him if he knows the difference between the truth and a lie. The child replies, "Gosh, yes! Everybody knows you shouldn't tell a lie—especially in court!" And the movie-set courtroom audience titters with laughter.

But someone made that up. And, truth to tell, it isn't nearly as funny as the following, which, I assure you, are not made up. Notice, in this first example, that the RA does not listen to the answer to his first real question:

Q. Johnny, I'm going to ask you some questions now and I want all of your answers to be oral, okay?
A. Okay.
Q. What school do you go to?
A. Oral.
Q. What grade are you in?
A. Oral.

*****

In this next exchange the witness knew what she knew and, by golly, she knew how important what she knew was:
Q. What do you think God would do to you if you didn't tell the truth?
A. Send me to my room.[76]

*****

In the following exchange the witness likewise had figured out something important about the application of this OATH thing:
Q. Now, Bobby, if we let you swear on the Bible that you will tell the truth, the whole truth and nothing but the truth, and then you tell a lie, do you know what would happen to you?

---

[76]When the folks of my generation were children and our parents said, "Go to your room," it was a "terrible penalty. Now when a [parent] says the same thing, a kid goes to his room. There he's got [air conditioning, television, VCR, stereo]—he's better off than he was in the first place." (A modified version of a Sam Levenson quote from the 1960s.)

A. Yes, sir. I'd be kicked out of Cub Scouts.

*****

I am led to believe that in the following exchange the judge was rather obviously gruff, a character trait often observed in judges:

Q. Now, then, young man, do you attend church or Sunday school?
A. No, sir.
Q. Well, then, do your parents have a Bible in the house?
A. No, sir.
Q. Do you know who God is?
A. I don't think so, sir.
Q. Do you mean you don't know who created the universe?
A. (After a long pause) You?

THE RECORD (mine, at least) does not reflect whether the judge admitted or denied that allegation. Or supposition. Or whatever.

*****

The following is both instructive and provocative, from the actual testimony of a nine year-old:

Q. Henry, do you remember what I told you about testifying today? Do you remember I talked to you about being on the witness stand?
A. Yes.

Q. What did I tell you was the most important thing to do? Do you remember what I said about telling the truth?

A. Yes.

Q. What did I tell you about that? What did I tell you, Henry?

A. To sit up straight.

My guess is the kid had total recall and would have spoken sooner had the lawyer allowed it with a moment of non-speech. Why is that we always tell kids to sit up straight anyway?

*****

And then there is little Jenny, whose wisdom far exceeded her years:

Q. Jenny, do you know what happens if you tell a lie in court?

A. Uh huh. You go to hell?

Q. Is that all?

A. Isn't that enough?

For me it's enough. For this chapter anyhow.

20

IS IT REAL OR IS IT MEMORY?

You never know how much a person can't remember until that person is called as a witness.

—Laurence J. Peter

By now you have come to realize that Truth in the practice of law is stranger than fiction, funnier than jokes. A recurrent theme in RA-witness exchanges is the inability of the witness to remember something—the MT (previously referred to as the Memory Thing).

I personally have never thought of coffee as a memory enhancer, but the gentleman being deposed in the following exchange apparently felt otherwise:

Q. Mr. Campos, maybe we're having an arithmetic problem. Can you tell me how many years ago 1961 was? How many years ago was that?

A. 1961? To now? You want me to answer that question?

Q. If you can. If you can't, just say, I don't know.

A. Well, I can start thinking back and tell you. Be all right with you?

Q. Surely, take your time.

A. You got me without my coffee this morning....I'm used to getting up in the morning and getting coffee before I even say one word to my wife.

Q. Do you want to take a break and have some coffee?

A. Be a good idea.

Mr. Campos is said to have ordered cream, sugar, and a twentieth century calendar with his coffee.

*****

Lawyers who take depositions become accustomed to the MT. They encounter many witnesses with memory problems, often very select memory problems:

Q. Are you sure that's the only time you met with this woman?

A. I have a little bit of loss of memory since I was in this car accident...in 1964, but I may have met with her another time.

Q. Well..., did you lose your pre-1964 memory or do you just have a memory problem since then.

A. I may have a memory problem since then, but maybe not. I think I met her one other time, but I can't say for sure, you know.

Q. Have you ever taken any medication or anything like that for a memory problem?

A. No.

Q. Am I the first person you have told about your memory problem?

A. I think so. Yeah.

Q. At least if you told anybody else, you can't remember?

A. Right.

The lawyer was heard to say later that he should have asked, "Would it be fair to say that you think you have a memory problem, but you just can't remember what it is?"

*****

And in this next example, the witness clearly remembered what had happened, but, being the victim of the lawyer's apparent hearing impairment, was almost held to have stated that something else had happened:

Q. Why would you be living in the east part of Dallas and be going to Sunset [High School] in Oak Cliff?

A. Because I couldn't attend Skyline High School anymore, which is where I was going.

Q. Why not?

A. Because I had been late a few times and—

Q. You had been laid?

A. Been late for school.

Q. Oh, boy, am I glad you cleared that up!

*****

And speaking of clearing things up, in the following example the lawyer's mind was on cruise control, but there was some disconnection between the eyesight's reading of the notes and the muscles' activation of the vocal chords. This is from a hearing in a dental malpractice case, having something to do also with a "negligent referral case of an oral surgeon":

Counsel 1: Plaintiff's counsel takes the position that in a negligence case, and in this case in particular, that if Dr. Ryan ever learned anything, he should have learned that he was not able to perform oral sex. Let's take that situation—

    Judge: Excuse me?

    Counsel 1: I'm sorry. Oral surgery.

    Counsel 2: I'm glad we're having a record today.

    Counsel 1: I've got it written down as "SX." I'm sorry, Judge. Thank you. I didn't even know I said it....

    For THE RECORD, Counsel 1 and 2 were Mr.'s. The judge was a Ms. And the word *sex* was never uttered by Perry Mason in mixed company.

21

THE IMPORTANCE OF APPEARANCES

*It is not truth that makes man great
but man who makes truth great.*

—Confucius

In previous chapters I have said a lot about THE OATH—that thing that witnesses "take" before they set out to tell the Truth and so forth in court or in a deposition. My study of sworn testimony has led me to believe that once THE OATH is administered, some witnesses, in the best of faith, go totally bonkers. The exchanges which follow involve adults only. Adults who did not plead loss of memory. There are no childish excuses for these answers, or these questions!

Appearances can be deceiving:

Q. Mrs. Jones, is your appearance this morning pursuant to a deposition notice which I sent to your attorney?

A. No. This is how I dress when I go to work.

*****

But appearance is often important. If not to the lawyer, then to the witness:

Q. Have you had an opportunity to prepare for this deposition today?

A. I took a shower and cleaned up.

It is said that when the witness was casually asked by the deposing lawyer what he planned to do "now that the deposition is over," he relied, "Take another shower."

*****

The concept of "appearance" may be understood on multiple levels:

Q. Have you ever appeared as a witness in a suit before?

A. Yes.

Q. Please tell the jury what suit it was.

A. It was a blue suit, with white collar and cuffs and white buttons all the way down the back.

*****

And even that which does not appear to be an appearance may seem like an appearance to the witness:

Q. Did you have your seat belt on at the time of the accident?

A. No, but I had my girdle on.

*****

In the following exchange it is possible that the questioning attorney wished that he had put in at least one less appearance in at least one location:

Q. Officer, do you have a nickname?
A. Yes, sir. I believe I am known as 'Bear.'
Q. Where did you get that nickname?
A. Well, I believe you gave it to me the last time I threw you in jail for being drunk.

*****

Then sometimes, it is not so much the appearance that counts, but the appearance of an appearance:
COUNSEL: Note our exception, Your Honor, and we would like the court to have an in camera observation of [the witness's notes].
WITNESS: There ain't no camera up here and I ain't got no pictures.
I mean, how could they take a picture of something that hadn't yet appeared?

*****

In the next example, somebody needed some witnesses to appear:
Q. You say you're innocent, yet five people swore they saw you steal the watch.
A. Your Honor, I can produce 500 people who didn't see me steal it.
And probably thousands who didn't see a thing.

*****

And in this next example the appearance of the arresting officer clearly made an impression on the defendant:

A. The subject was an elderly female. She was still in her car, with the motor running, and the car was off the road and straddling a large log with all four wheels off the ground and spinning.

Q. Patrolman Smith, what led you to suspect that the defendant was intoxicated?

A. I climbed up on the log and knocked on her window, which was closed. She rolled the window down and gave me a strange look and then looked at her speedometer...and said, "How can you be keeping up with me? I'm doing 40 miles an hour!"

According to THE RECORD, the defendant shortly thereafter changed her Innocent plea to Guilty. Or something like that.

22

ON SERIOUSNESS AND SPONTANEITY

*What plays the mischief with the truth is
that men will insist upon the universal
application of a temporary feeling or opinion.*

—Herman Melville

About these chapter prescripts[77]: As an English major, I feel compelled occasionally to justify the price my parents paid for my undergraduate education (in English literature) by dropping in the spontaneous, yet serious, literary quote ("SYSLQ"). For, in trial and deposition settings, serious spontaneity and spontaneous seriousness go hand in glove. With Truth, their ever-constant companion.

As an attorney-writer, I have been unabashed at revealing the Truth in the practice of law. Emphasizing right along that Truth is more entertaining than lawyers as lizard meals (*Jurassic Park*), lawyers who leave Harvard believing that their employers will lease them expensive new automobiles and pay off their student loans (*The Firm*), and other fiction that is dominating the large screen of late.

---

[77]My fancy little name for the fancy little quotes at the beginning of each chapter. Some folks call them *epigraphs*, but that sounds too grave for me.

In this first example, even though he may not have correctly understood the question, the witness seriously and spontaneously gave the right answer:
Q. *Have you been frank in your answers?*
A. *No, I've been telling the truth.*
At least he didn't say, "No, I've been earnest." Okay, so maybe that is not quite as funny as Mitch McDeere's entry into the Witness Protection Program!

*****

But consider the following three-way exchange among trial court, defense counsel, and accused:
Judge: Is the defendant known by any other names?
Ms. F: Do you have an a.k.a.?
Defendant: Hell, lady, I don't even have a car.
Now, that is serious spontaneity.

*****

Speaking of cars, here's another spontaneous exchange in a different context—an accident case in which the plaintiff had wrecked his father-in-law's automobile. The father-in-law, himself a lawyer, was present at the deposition:
Q. *You don't have any current complaints of pain or injury that you relate to this accident, do you?...*
A. *No....*
Q. *There's nothing you can't do today that you could do before this accident?*
A: *I can't borrow his car.*

*****

There's a bit of spontaneity in the following exchange as well:

A. . . . That outfit is headed by a guy that I don't like.
Q. Is that Mr. Smith?
A. That's Mr. Smith.
Q. Do you know where Mr. Smith is today?
A. I hope he's in hell, but I don't know. I can't confirm it.

*****

And then there was a woman who, seriously, was not about to tell a lie about her marriage:

Q. What is your name?
A. Ernestine McDowell.
Q. What is your marital status?
A. Fair.

A fair answer, if you ask me.

*****

This exchange is from an annulment proceeding, in which the female witness was spontaneously obliged to tell of a most romantic marriage proposal:

Q. Now, would you like to tell the judge what really happened when you married him?
A. First of all, I didn't marry him, he married me. Secondly, he went with me to the courthouse to check on the title to my property. When we got through he said, "Let's stop by the County Clerk's Office." And I said,

"What for?" And he said, "Well, you said you ain't gonna have no one lolling around your house without some legal papers."

Judge: Is this the reason you want an annulment, because he was lolling around your house?

A. That's the trouble, Judge. He just couldn't loll.

*****

The following is from the deposition of a naturalized citizen, who was doing the best he could to master the English language, as spoken by Americans. And to avoid being seriously confused by the goings on:

Q. Why didn't you file your tax return for 1990?

A. There is a reason for it.

Q. I figured there probably is, and that's why I'm asking you. What is the reason?

A. I did not receive my 10-W-40.

A heavyweight answer from a slippery witness.

But even the foreigner in the above example may not have been as spontaneously confused as the eyewitness in the next example, who was described as an "elderly gentleman from Jamaica":

Q. Now, Mr. Augustine, while you were watching, at this time you didn't know of anything unusual going on, did you?

A. No, not—

Q. Okay. So you were just sitting in your yard casually watching what was going on in the neighborhood?

A. Well, I wasn't watching, but I was seeing. I was just seeing what was going on, because it was all in front of my eyes and I could remember what I seen is what I

*saw. I won't say what I didn't saw. What I seen is just
what I saw. Whatever I say I see is just what I did saw.*
How'd you like to conjugate some verbs with that
guy?[78]

*****

The following exchange occurred during cross-
examination of a government worker who had issued a
citation for a *serious* violation of a health and safety
statute. The degree of *seriousness*, as stated in the citation
itself (by use of the word showcased below), was at issue:
*Q. Could you define the word blatant for me,
please?*
A. I believe it is something that sheep do.
And when they do it, I am told, they do it blatantly.

*****

In terms of seriousness and spontaneity, however,
I doubt there has ever been a witness to surpass the
deposition performance of the Winstead's employee, from
Corpus Christi, especially where making THE RECORD
is concerned:

---

[78]In fairness (?), the lawyer who initially interviewed this
witness reported that when he went to the man's home, "he was
sitting in a lawn chair in the front yard across the street from the
scene of the offense,...drinking a Heineken...and had three or
four empties around him."

Q. ...Where are you working now?

*A. ...I'm employed at Winstead's in Corpus Christi.
And I am a fashion consultant. Not a saleslady; a fashion
consultant for men. And I want all of you all's cards. Do
not forget to give them to me. And I'm the best, too. I sold
$218,614 this year—yeah, that's how much I sold this year.
And October 31st was the end of our year. Let that be on
the record, Honey, because that was a record! They eat it
up. And I get paid—do you want to know how much I get
paid, Honey? Six dollars an hour, six days a week. But you
know what? I manage very well, do you think?*

Q. I expect you do.

A. And I don't do any whoring, either.

No one quite knew what to say after that remark. It
is obviously a chapter ender.

23

COLOR ME CANDID

The truth is more important than the facts.
—Frank Lloyd Wright

In the chapter last past I wrote about seriousness. And how it and Truth go together—like birds of a feather flocking together. Especially in real life, where witnesses and their testimony are concerned. Yet another element, however, is so often present with these two: candor.

I don't know what feathered the sentiment of the woman whose testimony appears in the next example, but I've a deep down type of feeling that she was being serious, true, and candid:

A. ...I couldn't do a damn thing with [my husband.] He beat the hell out of me, and I divorced him.

Q. And when did you divorce him, please?

A. God, I don't know. I closed that out of my mind. I mean I threw that S.O.B. in the garbage can and stomped it way down and then took it in a helicopter and dropped it in the middle of the ocean.

Figuratively speaking, we hope.

*****

The following is from the candid deposition testimony of the supervisor of a chronically absent school district employee. The accent—which can be detected even as one reads this testimony—is unmistakably Southern:

A. ...*I have knowed of him missing a full week and people a-calling me,...onto me all of the time. Now, I have talked to [him] and we'd get it worked out that he would never do it again. Then he would do the same thing, over and over and over...and I'd lie to the school board just like a pure dog, and they knowed I was lying to them.*[79]

Which raises the issue: If everybody knowed it was a lie, did it not then, on some philosophical level, become

---

[79]This reference to a "pure dog lie" offers the opportunity, footnotewise, to bring in yet another candid falsehood exchange—this, however, from a trial, in which the divorce litigant's deposition was used against him:

Q. How much education do you have?

A. About three semesters at Lon Morris Junior College.

Q. Do you remember giving your deposition in my office several weeks ago?

A. Yes....

Q. Do you remember my asking you about your education at that time?

A. I think so....

Q. You stated you had a master's degree in geophysics from the University of Texas, didn't you?

A. Yes, sir.

Q. Mr. Chappell, when you gave that answer, were you mistaken or was it just a barefaced lie?

A. It was just a barefaced lie.

the functional equivalent ("FE") of the Truth, in which case it might, therefore [SLAP! SLAP!]—oh, forget it!

*****

The witness's accent in the next excerpt is universal, in my opinion. And the candor of the witness is compelling:

Q. Where do you physically reside?

A. It depends on the night?

Q. Where do you physically reside on Monday nights?

A. It depends on how I feel.

*****

Why don't you try to guess the accent of this next fellow, whose testimony is, without doubt, totally candid:

Q. Okay. How long does it take you to get from where you live to Mr. Hicks' office in Mt. Vernon?

A. From where I live it's fourteen miles to Mt. Pleasant, fourteen miles to Pittsburgh, and fourteen miles to Mt. Vernon. I am fourteen miles from nowhere any which way I go and that's another fourteen to come home—that's twenty-eight miles throwed away.

Once again proving there's no place like home.

*****

But perhaps the following example demonstrates an even greater degree of candor on the part of a witness who, one would think, might have had a certain degree of exposure with regard to his testimony:

Q. Were you checking into a room at the hotel?

A. Yes.

Q. For what reason?

A. Well, the girlfriend I had living in my house wasn't going to like that one that I had with me that night.

Let's hope neither of the girlfriends got their hands on that guy's deposition.

*****

In keeping with what may seem to be a theme, here's another exchange from a woman with few regrets about her changed situation in life:

Q. Are you married?

A. No, I'm divorced.

Q. What did your husband do before you divorced him?

A. A lot of things I didn't know about.

Perhaps at least some of this stuff is more humorous than the insurance lawyer in *Jurassic Park* getting scarfed up by a dinosaur.

*****

But I must be candid and say that I do not believe the next excerpt is in any way funny. It is *comedic* in a tragic sense. But not funny! So don't laugh.

Q. Now, Mr. Russell, Mrs. Russell said that you hit her so hard that you knocked her from the dining room into the kitchen. Is that true?

A. *That's a damn lie. I hit her so hard she dropped right where she was—out cold.*

*****

Nor do I think the next excerpt is funny. I offer it merely because of its educational potential:

A. *I guess I need this divorce on—I think you call it unreconcilable differences. She reconciled with somebody else.*

Now that was a candid response, truthful and serious. And the guy was representing himself, so there really was no *question* as such. So, perhaps it was not even a *response* as such.

*****

In the following example, there unmistakably was a question as such:

Q. *Just what did you do to prevent this accident?*

A. *I closed my eyes and screamed as loud as I could.*

Bad question. Good answer.

*****

The following non-candid testimony is from a Labor Court proceeding, in which a lamp shade company employee was challenging his dismissal for using profanity on the job.

A. *Well, your honor, my colleague was soldering some wires close to the ceiling and I was holding the ladder. He was not paying attention to the solder that fell, and I complained more than once. At a given point in time, on purpose, he let fall onto my shoulder a red-hot piece of metal.*

Q. (Judge, interrupting) And at that very moment, what did you say?

A. I said, "Look here, dear colleague, at the hole you have made in my shirt."

The people who overheard his remark and complained to management should be ashamed.

*****

Speaking of labor law, the following is from a Labor Court proceeding in Brazil:

Q. Mr. Manuel, the claimant says that he worked a minimum of two overtime hours per day. Is that true?

A. Your Honor, deep down inside it is true, but he'll never get any witnesses to prove it.

So I think I am ready to elevate candor to the same level as Truth and seriousness (though neither seriousness nor candor are yet worthy of capitalization).

*****

You will find the candor of the witness in the following to be exemplary:

Q. How do you make a living when you are not in jail?

A. Stealing.

Q. That's what got you in this trouble in the first place, isn't it?

A. I ain't very good at it.

Compare the foregoing, if you will...

*****

...with the following, in which the witness lacked all vestiges of candor:

Q. Did you stay all night with this man in New York?

A. I refuse to answer that question.

Q. Did you stay all night with this man in Chicago?

A. I refuse to answer that question.

Q. Did you stay all night with this man in Miami?

A. No.

Not candid. She'd probably never even been to Miami.

*****

Candid:

Q. James stood back and shot Tommy Lee?

A. Yes.

Q. And then Tommy Lee pulled out his gun and shot James in the fracas?

A. Uh, no sir. Just above it.

*****

Overly candid:

A. The accident happened on the fifteenth day of December.

Q. Well, how do you fix that date?

A. Mister, I didn't fix the date. The Lord God Almighty fixed that date!

*****

Complete candor:

Q. I take it that before this accident happened you lived with your brother-in-law and sister for about six months?

Q. Yes.

Q. You got to know him quite well?

A. Yes.

Q. And you saw him interact with your sister, and I believe they have one child?

A. I didn't see the actual interaction, but they did have one child.

Had he seen the interaction, could he have been arrested as a peeping Tom brother-in-law?

*****

More complete candor:

A. [The only other accident I've been involved in] was when I was driving down this logging road in a pickup truck and ran into a hog.

Q. Was anyone hurt?

A. Only the hog.

Q. Was he hurt bad?

A. He must have been, because he died.

*****

Candor here? You decide:

Q. How are you employed?

A. Ranger Boat, or Wood Manufacturing. You can go either way.

Q. Maybe it can, and I want to confess to you now that I'm not as smart as most of these other lawyers here, so, if I do this too slow for you, please be patient with me. Are you employed by Ranger Boat, or by Wood Manufacturing?

A. I'm in the trailer shop, but the products come to them in either name. They get their products either addressed to Wood Manufacturing, or to Ranger Boat. They answer to either, but I'd say Ranger Boat.

Q. Who signs your paycheck, Ranger Boat or Wood Manufacturing?

A. Randy Hopper signs my paycheck.

*****

You be the judge of the candor of this testimony of a promoter who was charged with creating a "Ponzi scheme" of investments, whereby past investors were repaid with later investors' money:

Q. And so, is there presently a producing oil well on that prospect lease?

A. Yes, of course, we have a brand new oil well on that lease.

Q. And when did you drill this "brand new" oil well?

A. 1985.

Q. But this is 1988.
A. Yes, it has been brand new for three years.
But what about the warranty?

*****

And then sometimes candor can be painful. As reflected by the following testimony from the plaintiff in a malpractice case against the hospital in which her spouse, a fundamentalist preacher, spent his final days. And, according to her sworn statements, they were not especially good days:

Q. Why did your husband write notes?
A. He couldn't talk.
Q. How many pages of notes do you have?
A. ...two or three, and my daughter has got one or two, and we threw some of them away....
Q. But you decided to keep some of them.... Why did you decide to keep some of them? Was there some special meaning to them?
A. Yes.
Q. What kinds of things did you keep notes about?
A. One I have he told us on Sunday before he passed away the next Sunday, he wrote, "The King is coming. You all stay in church." And, naturally, that meant something, and I kept it.
Q. Did any of them have to do with any criticism that he had of the care he was getting or anything like that?...
A. Well, one of them, he couldn't make us understand. He kept trying to tell us something. And he

wrote, "Want the doctor." And finally he wrote on there: "Ass hole."

Q. *And who did you take that to be referring to?*

A. *It was his rectum! And that's what he was wanting to see the doctor for!*

That seems an appropriate excerpt on which to *end* this chapter.

24

MISTAKES THAT GIT MADE

The brain is as strong as its weakest think.

—Eleanor Doan

Perhaps the one area in which the Fleming Act is not likely to bring about enhanced sensitivity on the part of the non-legal public is non-court communication. That is, the arena in which RAs communicate back and forth with their assistants and with other lawyers. It is difficult at this time to weigh the problematical aspect of this shortcoming. For it is in this arena that some of the wildest concepts emerge through the double-barrelled shotgun of *word processos* (or *computeros*)[80] and malapropisms.[81]

---

[80]Formerly known as *typos*, short for typographical error.

[81]The distinction between a word *processo* and a malapropism is that a *processo* occurs as a result of the phenomenon that, from time to time (and frequently), although the operator of the machinery knows what he or she intends to type, the machine in question (be it typewriter, word processor, or computer) comes out with something else. A malapropism, however, is an error resulting from a person's intending to write or say exactly what comes out on the printed page or what issues forth from the vocal chords.

Assuming you just read the most recent Clever
Footnotes, I now am in a position to assume that you know
and appreciate the two basic concepts with which I will
deal in this chapter. RAs must train themselves, or allow
others to train them, to be good proofreaders. However,
inevitably there are occasional breakdowns in even the best
of established processes. As a challenge to the reader I
shall allow you to decide whether the examples which
follow are word processos or malapropisms.[82]

---

[82]By the way (and once again to justify the price of my
undergraduate education), the word *malaprop* became accepted
as a noun around 1823. It derives from a character, Mrs.
Malaprop, in Irish playwright R.B. Sheridan's *The Rivals,* a
1775 comedy. A malaprop is a misapplication of a word for one
with similar sound or meaning, usually with a humorous result.
Among the gems produced by Mrs. Malaprop:
   "I would have her instructed in geometry, that she might
know something of the contagious countries" (Act I, sc. ii);
   "[W]e will not anticipate the past,...our retrospection
will now be all to the future" (Act IV, sc. ii);
   "Here's fine suicide, paracide and simulation going on
in the fields! and Sir Anthony not to be found to prevent the
antistrophe" (Act V, sc. i); and
   "[I]f I reprehend anything in this world, it is the use of
my oracular tongue, and a nice derangement of epitaphs" (Act
III, sc. iii).
   For some strange reason, a decade or so after *malaprop*
became accepted folks began to add *ism* to *malaprop*, thus
creating a word to mean basically the same thing that was
already completely covered by an existing word. *See*
WEBSTER'S NINTH NEW COLLEGIATE DICTIONARY (1983).

*****

The portion of a complaint which asks (or prays or demands) damages from the defendant carries the time-honored name the *ad damnum*. Following a lengthy discourse to the effect that opposing counsel's request for damages was excessive, an RA of my acquaintance is alleged to have stated to the other RA: "The *jest* of the matter is that the *addendum* in your Complaint is ridiculous!"

*****

A former assistant of mine once produced the following from my dictation: "The Rulc of Thum in such a matter is to...." (She had previously transcribed a number of briefs in which I had made references to some other RA Rules that occasionally get capitalized—the Rule Against Perpetuities[83] and the Rule in Shelley's Case.[84]

---

[83]In keeping with the haphazard scholarship displayed from time to time in other areas of this work, for the benefit of the non-lawyer reader, the Rule against Perpetuities is a common law principle to the effect that an interest in property is void unless it must vest no later than 21 years, plus a nine-month (or slightly longer) period of gestation, after one or more human lives in being at the time of the attempted creation of the interest. If you do not understand this Rule from the definition here given, you are in the company of most of the judges in this country.

*****

A veteran court reporter produced the following, transcribing a bank officer's deposition:

Q. What documents had you prepared in conjunction with the proposed...transaction?

A: An agreement for a Stopple[85] and a Warranty Deed.

The witness was not asked what size or brand of Stopple the agreement was for.

*****

A court reporter produced the following as well:

Q. And your lawyers let you publish a statement like that?

A. Our lawyers looked at the draft report and no one had a problem with it.

Q. You must not have any good lawyers.

A. *Good lawyers*...That's a Nazi moron, right?

I understand at least one of the lawyers involved in this deposition took exception to the reporter's interpretation of "oxymoron."

---

[84]This is another common law property rule, "an antique feudal doctrine" which, unlike the Rule Against Perpetuities, has been abolished by statute in most states. In keeping with the haphazardness of scholarship displayed from time to time in this work, I am opting not to elaborate further on this rule.

[85]For the non-lawyer reader, the witness had in mind an "estoppel agreement."

*****

A similar error of transcription of an unfamiliar word has been known, on more than one occasion, to produce an exchange of the following sort:

Q. You have admitted, have you not, to engaging in an adulterous relationship with this young lady during the time that you were still legally married to my client?

A. Yes, sir.

Q. What I want to know is this: At what point in time did this adulterous relationship commence between you and your power mower?

A high energy relationship, if you ask me.

*****

I've never yet figured out just where the breakdown occurred in the following exchange:

Q. Do you drink?

A. Well, not at the moment. I've been sober now going on three years. But before that I used to drink fluently.

Hey, it's an international language for some folks.

*****

I once proofread a letter in which I was trying to nudge a defense lawyer into a reasonable settlement, gasping when I came to this language: "This is the second time you have referred to this case as being an appropriate one to settle for the costs of the fence."

Since the case had nothing to do with walls or fencing, I felt certain that what I had dictated was "cost of defense." I attached a cliched note to my revision: "Deliver de letter, de sooner de better."

*****

In a letter I once received, another lawyer communicated with me about arrangements for my taking of her client's deposition: "As soon as I get aholt of my client, I will call you to set up a date and time."

The lawyer got aholt[86] of me on the phone the next day, as I recall.

*****

In following instance, one of my former trusted employees was typing a brief from notes I had written in longhand. I wished to point out certain characteristics of a case, commonly known as *distinctions*. She produced: "In the present case, there are two disfunctions."

The boss's handwriting was obviously one of them.

*****

---

[86]*See also* chapter 18, *supra*, in which the questioning lawyer therein used the preferable form of this word, *ahold*. *Don't see*, however, any dictionary for purposes of defining either word. Either you know the definition or you don't, and that's all there is to it!

Another former assistant may have had a slight problem reading her own handwriting. In a planning session for the week, as she took notes, I asked that she procure for me *file marked* copies of a document. Later in the day I almost signed a letter reading, "Please send me five more copies of the mortgage."

*****

Someone confessed to me that the following was done so hurriedly, in a last-minute addendum to documents essential to a real estate closing, that the lawyers did not catch the mistake until months following the closing: "The parties acknowledge that the buyer's *right to reject* a portion of the assets was exercised; accordingly, the purchase price was reduced and the closing documents were amended to reflect the exercise of this *writer projection.*"

One of the lawyers, believing himself to be the only "writer" at the closing was most despondent for several days—feeling, he said, that he either had been rejected or was in the process of projecting.

*****

I shall never forget receiving a copy of an opposing RA's letter to a judge and reading these words: "I would like to take this opportunity to *capsize* my client's case."

Recalling the results, I wish the guy's case had been capsized before it went to the jury.

*****

Occasionally, the word processor will have a Freud-
ian aroma. For instance, in a letter to a colleague who had
taken the writer to his hometown lunch meeting at which
local lawyers discussed the cases in the *Advance Sheets*,[87]
this transcription occurred: "I appreciate your taking me to
the most educational session of the Advanced Speech
Committee."

*****

Pursuant to an affiliation with a writers' association
in Arkansas, for several years I read and judged essays that
were supposed to be brief, witty, and about law, business,
or politics. An outstanding (and award-winning) entry one
year was "We Have Burned Our Britches Behind Us" by
Patricia McRaven.

The author told of a heartbreaking memo from the
boss: "You shouldn't drink alcohol because...it gives you
psoriasis of the liver." And of a public transportation
customer who wrote the transit authority about his
displeasure at having to transfer buses on the way to work:
"I am a person who likes to stay on the bus until I reach
my destiny."

---

[87]"Advance Sheets" is a nickname given to softbound
publications of court decisions, which are published and
distributed regularly. The word "advance" is used because these
publications precede the publication of the same cases in hard-
bound volumes. The Advance Sheets publication for the
Arkansas appellate courts is called the "Arkansas Advance
Reports."

My favorites from Patricia's essay were attributed to an acquaintance who tried to impress the author by claiming to have read all of *Shakespeare's books*. He was especially fond of the poems of Edgar Allen *Pope*. And from the Romantic era, he gave high marks to "Byron's 'Imitations of Immorality.'" The essayist astutely noted, "Where Byron was concerned, those were not imitations."

*****

And then there was the following exchange of correspondence in which I engaged sometime in 1990. Thanks to the modern miracle known as the fax machine, this exchange occurred in full in less than one hour. In a "FAX MEMO" I wrote opposing counsel,

> My client advises that while he was at lunch today, Messrs. Linder and Tucker [former employees] entered the premises of my client's place of business and defiantly removed company records that my client had specifically told them were not to be removed because they were company records....

Within minutes I received a response over the wire, acknowledging receipt of the memo, denying any wrongdoing, and elaborating:

> I am advised that Messrs. Linder and Tucker only removed documents that they were entitled to and did so on advice of

counsel. This was done without objection or breach of the peace. Additionally, my clients are entitled to other documents, as well as certain personal items, that remain on the penises and want to know when they can pick them up. We would be happy to have a hearing concerning these matters.

I absolutely refuse to comment on what, if anything, I had to say to opposing counsel and/or his assistants regarding the proposed hearing on the issue of the gentlemen's being able to pick up the items that remained on the penises. I was told, however, that the transcriptionist (of his handwriting or dictation) was one embarrassed female for the remainder of the day.

Even in the later longer "Perry Mason" shows, fax machines never entered the picture.

25

SLANGUAGE AND WORDIFICATION

Slang is a language that rolls up its sleeves,
spits on its hands and goes to work.
—Carl Sandburg

Another potential problem, pertaining to the overall effect of the Fleming Act, is that an RA's world is fraught with picturesque "slanguage." Which is to say that, both historically and presentically, lawyers and judges create not only phrases but also words to meet the needs at hand. Some figurative, some not so figurative.

We have *books* that police and prosecutors *throw* at folks. Yet no one ever really picks up a volume of literature and heaves it in the direction of another person.

We have money that gets left on *the table* in circumstances where there was no table to begin with. We have *smoke-filled* rooms, even when the participants therein are all non-smokers.

In cases where illegal evidence is used, we have *fruit from the poisonous tree.* That's right: no tree, no fruit.

We have *cows* that yearn to *eat forbidden cabbage.* No bovine. No veggies.

We have *wells that run dry* and *wells to which we cannot go too often*. No hole in the ground. No bucket. No water.

We *bite the bullet*, as well as *the hand that feeds us*. We get only *one bite at certain apples*. No bullet. No hand. No apple. No teeth.

And we have *dogs that won't hunt*. Like P.J and Little Thunder Jim. With one exception: no dogs.

All in the courtroom and in our law offices.

The use of figurative words and phrases does not necessarily come easy to the practitioner. And it is difficult for the non-lawyer to ingest this crucial fact of legal life. More than a passing degree of study is involved to attain proficiency.

*****

The legal world has its own brand of oxymorons. But no Nazi morons, that I know of. An oxymoron is a conspiracy between two or more words to make a sensible phrase with literal contradictions of terms. Classic examples are *slow speed, sweet sorrow, deafening silence,* and *terribly happy.*[88]

---

[88]In these days of the super-bureaucracy we also have multi-word phrases that boggle the most reasonable of minds. In 1983 I checked in at Washington, D.C., National Airport for a flight back to Little Rock, Arkansas. I was told it had been canceled. Not to worry, however, I was told at the airline desk, for my flight was going to "reoriginate" in St. Louis. To which the airline would fly me to catch the reoriginated flight. I decided not to show my ignorance about this concept of "reorigination."

Legal oxys include *divorce proposal, friendly dispute,* and, in certain courtrooms, *Your Honor.* The world of law evokes much "paranomasia," a/k/a *puns.* A pun is a play on words. A biblical example of a pun is Jesus' statement, "Thou art Peter (Petros), and upon this rock (petra) I will build my church."[89]

Legal puns include *misconceptions* in paternity cases, *appealing* attorneys in the Supreme Court, and my children's futile search of my closets for the *suits* I won last year.[90]

Not gonna ask, I said to myself. *Wouldn't be prudent.* I was determined to experience this concept without making a fool of myself by saying, "Uh, 'scuse me, m'am, but what is this 'reorigination' bidness all about?" It occurred to me that because the flight had been canceled before its scheduled take-off, without prior notice to passengers, and because the "reoriginated" flight was taking off at a later time in a different city, I was really dealing with a complex situation. As I pondered the matter across time zones, I shared with the flight attendants my conclusion that we were experiencing, firsthand, a *unilateral intercity time-delayed post-preorigination cancellation reorigination.* It took awhile to restore order to their ranks.

[89]*The Bible,* Matthew 16:18 (King James Version). It loses something in the translation from Greek to English.

[90]Please know that I am intentionally steering clear of contrived puns, instances wherein people have gone to some length to come up with a laughable word or combination. As an example, consider one reported in Peter MacDonald's *Court Jesters:* The witness, in a Canadian courtroom, had just testified

But the pun and oxymoron are by no means alone in the legal world.

There are numerous dead metaphors—those which are so firmly entrenched that the speaker and hearer no longer are aware that the words are not literal. Litigants have a "burden of proof." Lawyers "lead" their witnesses. Sometimes verdicts are "shocking to the conscience of the court." Plaintiff's cases are said to "survive" motions to dismiss.

Redundancy abounds. Despite pleas from all factions, even RAs seldom "say" things in pleadings. They *allege and state*. They do not let clients "leave" things to their heirs, but insist that they *give, devise and bequeath*. Real estate deeds continue to *grant, bargain, sell and convey* property; time periods in legal documents run *from and after* a particular date; and judgments are *had and recovered from and against* losing parties. And on and on.

Then, of course, there is the occasional ingenious use of a word that baffles all the listeners. The story is told of an attorney by the name of O'Connell who, in his summation to a jury, had used every conceivable "epithet of abuse" to describe the adversary. Stopping for an instant to think, he added, "This naufrageous ruffian." When

---

that he was a graduate of the University of Michigan Law School. The judge then asked, "Do you know Professor Bates?" To which the witness replied, "Yes, and I know his son, Master Bates."

friends later asked the meaning of the word, he confessed he did not know, but said he thought it sounded good.[91] Notwithstanding O'Connell's brilliance, the dictionaries to date don't admit that "naufrageous" is a word. But if there is one thing that RAs mustn't be afraid to do, it's add words to the language where appropriate. I call this process wordification. Without in depth elaboration, I take credit for the wordification of clarificational, foxacious, pocketify, stimulogenerational, shinky, trophetic, and Fuddruckerize, which, I assure you, are working their way into the dictionaries.

*****

DIGRESSIONALIZATION.
Fuddruckerize is the type of word that might prompt numerous fan letters, asking for further details. To avoid answering all those letters, I shall tell the story here and now.

Legal words are often created in unforeseeable ways. For instance, law enforcement personnel the world over know what it means to be "Mirandized," this word having been created by the U.S. Supreme Court case *Miranda v. Arizona*[92]

Lawyers speak ever so casually about "Brandeis briefs." Coined after the name of former Associate Justice

---

[91]*Modern Eloquence* (1900), volume X.

[92]384 U.S. 436 (1966).

Louis Brandeis, this phrase refers to briefs in which economic and social information are included with legal citations and principles.

In the wake of Senate hearings on one of former President Reagan's Supreme Court nominees, "to Bork" has become a legal verb, commemorating the manner in which the nominee failed to pass muster. These source allusions are intended to keep me from being "Bidened" (excoriated for casual plagiarism).

Some years ago I ran across a court decision that cried out to have part of its style become a legitimate word. In *Fuddruckers, Inc. v. Doc's B.R. Others, Inc.,*[93] a federal appeals court recognized that decor of premises and method of business may constitute protectable "trade dress" under the Lanham Act, which regulates trademarks and servicemarks. That is, in appropriate instances, an entity's ambiance may be entitled to the same protection as its logo.

Traveled readers will recognize Fuddruckers as a chain of trendy hamburger places. Based on what Doc's was alleged to have done, and shortly following the conclusion of a case in which my client prevailed on the theory for which the case stands, I proposed for the English language the verb *to Fuddrucker*, meaning to copy an establishment's trade dress with intent to profit.

I felt my proposal of this new verb would evoke many useful derivations—gerunds, participles, adjectives, etc. Given the legal origin, I thought, this line of words

---

[93] 826 F.2d 837 (9th Cir. 1987).

would surely crop up first and most frequently in court documents and, of course, the news media.

Plaintiffs' attorneys would plead generally that their clients were Fuddruckered, that a defendant committed the offense (unknown at common law) of Fuddruckering. In response to interrogatories, they would particularize the details of the alleged Fuddruckerization. They would seek cease and desist orders to compel an offending party to deFuddruckerate all premises in question.

Of repeat offenders, journalists would report that he reFuddruckered. An organized movement to stop offenders would be called anti-Fuddruckerites. Folks who feel Fuddruckering should be legalized would unite as counter-Fuddruckerites.

To date only *Fuddruckerize* has sustained its viability as a new word. And, as best I can tell, this is only in my personal vocabulary. Easy come, easy go. End of digressionalization.

*****

...You may find some of the referenced wordifications, as well as other new words that I have created, in other places in this book. Spot all of them; write them down on the back of a twenty dollar bill; and send it to me by December 31 of the year you in which you bought this book. Sooner or later thereafter, I'll send you a card and let you know how you did. Or I may have my mother send you the card. She discovered the manuscript of this book before I sent it off to the publisher. I caught it just before it hit the flames leaping from the fireplace.

POSTSCRIPT

Well, in the foregoing pages I have assayed to portray the Real World of Real Attorneys (previously referred to as "RAs")—in areas that do not come to light very often. It will be very important for you, the readers, to remember all that you have learned herein. For, in the not so distant future, you'll see me lobbying the Fleming Act through Congress. In memory and honor of Perry Mason, of course! And with the results of *People v. Simpson* in mind, as well.

When my lobbying efforts begin, no doubt one or more disbelieving Senators or Representatives will call for one or more polls on the issue of whether it is wise to pass a law that would discourage lawyer-bashing. They do this to get their constituents to show them which way the political wind is blowing on matters of importance. I will be counting on you to support the Lawyer Appreciation Act and to cite this book as your documentary research in support of your opinion.

Meanwhile, we must all go forward in the true spirit of Perry Mason, taking one day at a time, knowing that there is a possibility (however remote) that the Fleming Act may never become law. Which leads to the notion that hundreds of thousands of copies of this book should be circulated among the masses, so that the same message that would be conveyed by the Fleming Act apprenticeships might be gotten across to the target personnel in another fashion. *Amen.*

APPENDIX

FOREWORD
to *Real Lawyers Do Change Their Briefs*

The idea of humorous lawyers strikes most of us (even lawyers) as an oxymoron. Luckily for all of us, Victor A. (Vic) Fleming took on the challenge of exposing the funny bones in a profession that all too often takes itself far too seriously. But what more could be expected from a lawyer who officiated at the wedding ceremony of two golden retrievers? Probably that he has the clear eye to poke fun at all of us who labor in the legal system.

Vic, his wife Susan, and the undersigned became friends in the early 1980s. One of the undersigned was becoming Governor of Arkansas for the second time; Susan was becoming Little Rock's youngest (and first female) city manager; and Vic and the other undersigned were toiling in the trenches of legaldom.

Vic began his foray into humor on February 8, 1984, when a column entitled "Restoring the Image of Lawyers" appeared on the op-ed page of the *Arkansas Gazette*. Previously known for serious writing, Vic suddenly emerged as a satirist. That column was acclaimed by lawyers and non-lawyers alike. Thus was launched a campaign to portray the not so highly publicized world of Real Lawyers.

He solidified this campaign in October of 1984 with the christening of "Law, Literature & Laughter." This humor column has become one of the most popular features in the state bar's quarterly, *The Arkansas Lawyer* (ranking second behind "Disciplinary Actions"). As is evident from the pages of *Real Lawyers Do Change Their Briefs*, language and law are two of the author's great loves. When his wit is added to his knowledge of these two elements, the result usually is people laughing *with* each other and *at* themselves.

Placing before the reader more than a mere handful of humorous anecdotes, *Real Lawyers* portrays the little-known things that make the practice of law lively and fun.

This book is NOT FOR LAWYERS ONLY. *Real Lawyers'* analysis of the world of law practice should appeal to people who work for lawyers, people who have friends and neighbors who are lawyers, and, yes, even those who must claim lawyers as next of kin.

How does a collection lawyer respond when his adversary calls him an "old toad"? How does a lawyer diversify efforts to collect her fees? Can legal pleadings be written in poetry? How does a jury makes its decisions? Has an appellate court ever defined *hillbilly*? The answers to these and other questions await you hereinafter (a word lawyers use to mean "in the pages that follow").

Hillary Rodham Clinton
Bill Clinton
1989

ABOUT THE WRITER

Vic Fleming grew up in the 60s in a northwest Mississippi farming town. At Greenville High School he played four sports AND edited the sports section of the school paper, was in the National Honor Society AND edited the school literary magazine.

His mother encouraged him to study law. His father told him he'd do well as a professional speaker. So Vic became both, as well as a writer. At Davidson College his major was English, although his diploma is written in Latin. His law degree is from the University of Arkansas at Little Rock.

While practicing law and speaking, Vic also is a civil mediator and founder of the Center for Mediation and Dispute Resolution in Little Rock, Arkansas. He's the author of a weekly syndicated newspaper column, "I Swear." He teaches a class on Men's Energy at Second Presbyterian Church in Little Rock; coaches an Odyssey of the Mind team; and is a gourmet cook.

He lives in Little Rock with his spouse Susan and their two children, Elizabeth and Teddy.

OPPORTUNITY TIME (again)!

In case you didn't respond to the shameless solicitation at page 81 above, the folks at VAF "I Swear" Enterprises would still like to hear from you and fulfil your needs. Please use this page to order other of our products. Allow three weeks for delivery.

TO: VAF "I Swear" Enterprises

FROM:

_____

(Name)

_____

(Street Address)

_____

City, State, Zip Code)

Order Quantity Description   _____ Price

___ *Real Lawyers Do Change Their Briefs*   @7.95   ___

___ *Law, Literature & Laughter*   @5.95   ___

___ *Perry's Dead! (And the Juice is Loose)* @11.95   ___

___ "Restoring the Image of Lawyers"
        (audiotape)   @10.95   ___

Subtotal: _____
Add the greater of $2.00 or
5% postage and handling: _____

Total: _____

Checks payable to VAF "I Swear" Enterprises,
3801 TCBY Tower, Little Rock, Arkansas 72201

VAF "I SWEAR" ENTERPRISES
425 West Capitol, Suite 3801
Little Rock, Arkansas 72201
(501) 376-1152 / FAX (501) 372-3359

VICTOR A. FLEMING
BUSINESS SPEAKER & HUMORIST

Add motivational smiles to your next meeting. Vic's speeches are full of energy and educational humor. Consider these unsolicited remarks:

"I give you my highest compliments. Your speech was truly outstanding — informative and funny." M.K., Little Rock, Arkansas.

"... funniest thing I ever heard in my life." A.A., Jackson, Mississippi.

"I've spent three days listening to people rave about what a great talk you gave." K.L., Tulsa, Oklahoma.

"Your presentation was humor with a message, one of the most effective of all teaching devices." J.R., Scottsdale, Arizona.

"Your mix of humor with a message to maintain perspective was something we needed to hear." B.R., Little Rock, Arkansas.

SATISFACTION GUARANTEED
(by reimbursement of fee, no questions asked[94])

---

[94]But we've never had a complaint yet!

TOPIC MENU for Vic Fleming
ORAL PRESENTATIONS[95]

"Perry's Dead! (And the Juice is Loose)" — Legally Humorous Keynote that has never failed to please. Title and angle always customized to group's needs. A great banquet presentation. Vic's Most Requested!

"The Wizard of Ah's" — Keynote or Workshop about Internal Change and Creative Dispute Resolution. Educational, yet humorous, approach to dealing with change.

"The Secret is There is No Secret" — Creative Energy Channelling Workshop that emphasizes how to identify and use humor in the quest for deeper happiness at home and on the job.

"Don't Stay Lost." — On Creative Learning, Listening and Teaching. Create a more workable and more livable atmosphere, at the job and at home. Owning up to who, what, and where *you are* in order to be who, what, and where *you want.*

"Working with Companions Within" — On the Use of Archetype Energies — Warrior, Dreamer, Trickster and other archetypes are inside everyone. Understanding them can lead to positive and productive life habits.

---

[95]Sometimes known as speeches.

"Vic Fleming may have a Lot of Nerve, but he is, without question, a Very Witty Guy!"

-Judge Jerry Buchmeyer, Dallas, Texas

"Perry's Dead! is a great read for the legal and non-legal minded."

-Peter MacDonald, Q.C, Ontario Canada

"You'll be hearing from my attorney."

-Columnist Dave Barry, Miami, Florida